"Is That A Zombie?"

Peter Germany

For My Daughter

"Why is There a Body in the Boot?"

One

"Why is there a body in the boot?"

Bobby looked at Claire. He'd only gone into the restaurant to use the toilet. "Why'd you look in the boot? You know the job: pick the car up and drive it to the address we're given. Don't look in the boot. In fact, this job in particular specifically said, 'Don't open the boot', and what do you do? You open the damn boot."

"Alright, don't get your knickers in a twist. They won't know I looked."

"How do you know that? What if there's a microphone in here? What if they've got a sensor inside the boot? Fuck, for all we know we could be about to explode. Or they could plug it in and the car's computer will tell them that the boot was opened! The boot has an electronic release. You heard that story about the twat who was doing ninety up the M20 in his M3 cabriolet with a couple of tarts with him. He tried to put the roof down and it bent. He went into Beamer the next day, said the roof buckled. They phoned him up a few hours later and told him the roof had been activated at 2:33am while travelling at ninety-two miles per hour, which invalidated the warranty on his six month old penis compensator."

She smiled at him, "Do you really think there's a sensor to say when the back seats are folded down? And would we seriously let someone fuck us over? Come on, let's get going. I want to get over the twenty-five bridge before nine, and to be honest it might not be a body. It's just a huge bag that could fit a body."

"Well, we'd already be off and underway if you hadn't have looked in the boot!"

"If I give you a blowjob when we stop later, will you shut up?" She winked at him.

"Okay." Bobby smiled and went to pull away but an orange Focus ST flew by them and swerved to the left, reversing into the parking space next to them.

"Can't these pricks see it's one way? Arseholes." Bobby resisted the urge to blare the horn at them. Even if it wasn't a body in the boot, it was something that people didn't want attention drawn to. Discretion was key to a smooth run. Which made it strange they'd put it in a brand new bright white Range Rover, but the money had been especially good, so fuck it.

"Isn't that PJ's car?" Claire said.

She was right, it belonged to a neighbour of theirs.

" Yeah, let's get going. All we need is to be recognised in this white ego wagon. I fucking hate white cars."

Two

"They're doing this on purpose," Bobby said as they sat in traffic on the M25. "Ever since those twats at Highways England have been pushing for that second crossing the traffic here takes the piss. They got rid got of all the tolls which means it should go smoother but it's got worse. All because some dipstick wants to spend a ton of taxpayer's money which'll go to a company that pays off the twats in Westminster. They all just bend over backwards and let big business ass-fuck them, without lube."

"We need to get a swear jar for these journeys," Claire said. "And maybe have a time out period. Like where no one speaks for at least five minutes."

"Having a good rant is part and parcel of being British. If we can't have a good moan then it builds up and then the eruption isn't going to be a five minute clean up. And you know I've got a point. The government and their corporate masters won't be happy until Kent is just concreted over so from the coast to London it'll just be new-builds and fucking warehouses 'cause we don't make anything here anymore. Garden of England my arse, more like Back Yard of Britain. Fucking politicians."

"You're kinda sexy when you're ranting." Claire leant over and licked the side of his face, "but you need a shave, I hate the stubble."

"I know, I forgot to get some blades."

"Why do you think there's a body in the boot?"

"This again? Come on, Claire. There's a reason we get paid good money for what we do. We don't poke around. We get in the car, and drive it where we're told. Then we go home and fuck. Go on holiday, fuck some more. Then we chill and enjoy the shit out of life until the next job comes along. And let's be honest, it's likely not the first body we've transported, nor will it be the last."

"Yeah, I guess. Just curious."

"More likely bored. Grab your phone and read a bit, we ain't moving for a while."

Three

An hour later they saw why they weren't moving. There had been a crash, and only one lane open into the tunnels. There was an assortment of fire-engines, ambulances and police cars.

"If they start asking questions I'll rub your crotch, that'll throw 'em," Claire said.

"Although I'm not opposed to a good crotch rub, let's hope it doesn't get there."

Claire gave his crotch a little rub, he swatted her hand away and they laughed.

Slowly they edged closer to the scene of the accident. Three cars had become an automotive version of the Human Centipede while a lorry had hit a barrier and a motorbike was churned up under the lorry. A man in biker's leathers sat on the road with an oxygen mask over his face but he seemed in one piece.

"I bet he's shit himself," Bobby said as paramedics were performing CPR on a woman lying on the road near the Automotive Centipede.

"I reckon the biker was swerving in and out, as they do, and he changed lanes without looking properly, as they do; and the cars were all too close to each other and bang! The Corsa is getting spit roasted by the Audi and the Alfa."

"Bow chica vroom vroom," Claire added as they got past the accident and the lanes opened up for the tunnels under the River Thames at Dartford.

Bobby smiled a little as her accent slipped through. She worked hard on hiding it, but once in a while it came out.

Four

Once they were past the accident the traffic flowed and they were through the tunnel and past Lakeside in less time than a talentless wannabe took to have a sex tape "leaked" on the internet.

They drove in silence as Claire read and Bobby focused on the road. They'd never had an accident in the four years they'd been doing this and he was determined not to break that record today. Since he'd become an even more efficient outlaw. She grounded him in a way he'd never experienced before. He hadn't figured out how she did it, she just made him feel calmer.

The radio was playing Katy Perry's latest poppy track that Bobby actually liked. He found he was humming along to it when Claire broke his concentration.

"Have you been monitoring this thing in Prague?"

"A little, they were talking about locking the city down this morning,"

"They've done it, but locked the whole country down. Both the President and Prime Minister have resigned and there's a state of martial law in place, something about a virus spreading."

"Well, we knew that, a new Covid strain or something,"

"People are saying it's not that, it's something new. Some sort of biological weapon, highly contagious," she read on for a moment. "Apparently it makes people rabid,"

"Where's this all coming from? BBC, Sky News, Reuters?"

"Just personal accounts at the moment. Some dodgy footage, like the blurry stuff that is meant to show Bigfoot,"

"Until it's on the BBC it's all crap,"

"Yeah, because the BBC is a beacon of independent reporting and truth."

Five

Bobby buttoned his jeans up and gave his wife a long deep kiss. The services had been busy but they'd done enough of these runs to know where they could park in a busy car park and relieve a little tension without being caught or gathering spectators. Bobby was not one to perform with an audience, and Claire would have let him in a heartbeat if he'd even suggested it to her.

"What do you want?" He asked as they got out of the Range Rover.

"A double bacon XL large with a Coke, and a mocha if you get there first."

"Meet you at whatever coffee place is here." Bobby kissed her again and they both put their masks on. Covid was lived with now, but it let them wear masks without having someone wondering why they were hiding most of their faces.

They had their little routines, both went to the toilets. Bobby was always out first and would go and get the food. While he was doing that Claire would go into the Smiths - there was always a Smiths - and get some more snacks and energy drinks. That was when it became anyone's guess as to who would get to the Costa or Starbucks first. Today it was Claire but only just.

"There were two women in the ladies talking about this Prague thing, they seemed scared." Claire said, with a bag of snacks. They already had a holdall of goodies in the Range Rover but always forgot something or fancied something else. "Other people are talking as well, like worried talk."

"Probably just people who look for something to panic about.

"I think there's something to it." Claire gave their order to the barista, who spelt her name on the paper cup wrong, "This thing in Prague, apparently it's worse than everyone's been told and the Czech Government have been trying to hide and blag their way out of talking about it."

The mobile in Bobby's pocket rang. Not his iPhone, but the pay-as-you-go unregistered one. The one that had been delivered to them along with the Range Rover key and the vehicle's location.

"It's Smith, have you seen the reports from Prague?" The voice sounded amused but calm.

"We have."

"We believe it's genuine, but we expect you to deliver. Is that understood?"

"We will deliver,"

The line went dead.

"They're taking it seriously?" Claire said.

"Yep, they still expect us to deliver."

"Let's be a little more cautious then, just in case."

"Agreed," Bobby said. "We've got time, Birmingham isn't too bad. We'd already taken into consideration road works and so on, If this is something serious then it'll be a few hours before the government pull their noses out of each other's dirt boxes and even make a statement let alone do anything, and a few hours before people panic. We're good."

Six

They listened to the radio as they drove, BBC Radio 5live though. The government was telling people to be calm, it was all under control and there was no reason to worry. Video footage from mobile phones showed there was a lot to worry about.

Social media was saying the virus had got out of the Czech Republic and was spreading across Europe. Information was sketchy and unconfirmed, with most of the videos being very blurry and not showing much that would help. There wasn't any real proof from outside of the Czech Republic despite the rumours.

"If it is spreading, and we see cases of it here I'm not sure detouring is something we want to be doing," Bobby said. "The motorways will get busier but I think we could get bogged down in a town if we divert. It should be a last resort."

"I can see your point, but we know how chaotic the motorways get when it rains. Imagine what they'll be like when real panic takes hold. If we do have to come off the motorways and dual carriageways then let's try to steer clear of the towns and cities."

"What's going on here?" Bobby said as the traffic began to back up. "I can see blue lights up ahead." Bobby moved the Range Rover into the outside lane when a gap presented itself. "I've a feeling I need to be out of here."

Ten minutes, and a mile later, he was proved right as all but the outside lane were closed off. Bobby didn't look at the carnage, knowing he'd likely end up in the back of the van ahead of them if he did.

"That's three write-offs there at least."

"What do you think happened?"

"I'm not sure, six cars in all. Three totalled, maybe four. I doubt anyone has walked out of whatever type of car is in the middle there."

"Check the route on your phone, see what it's saying congestion wise. Also check Twitter, see what the people are saying on there."

"Already doing it."

Bobby started slowing the Range Rover as they passed the accident. They were already just crawling along but a little more caution wouldn't hurt.

"Traffic's looking clear, there's lots on Twitter across the country of people claiming they've seen people with this virus. Looking at our route I don't think we'll have a problem." She scrolled a little more, "There's reports coming from Edinburgh, and Liverpool now, but just that."

"Okay,"

They passed the accident and the cars started jilting into both lanes.

"Prague's a popular holiday location so people all over the country are going to have been there."

"Bigger the population and the bigger the chance there are people who will have been there recently," Bobby added as he passed a car that was doing 55mph. In his mirrors he saw something flying up fast behind him and put his foot down so he could move in front of the slower vehicle. A Mercedes flew past them. "He's doing at least a tonne thirty."

"All good and well until someone pulls out in front of him," Claire said not taking her gaze from her phone.

On the London bound carriageway five police cars went the other way at high speed.

"We're going to get a lot of that tonight," Bobby said.

"What the fuck was that?" Claire said and turned to see the explosion behind them.

"Read about it on the news later, I'm not hanging about here to find out."

Seven

Forty-five minutes passed without incident, but word of the virus spreading was escalating with reports from London and the South-East coming out. Their route was looking clear of these rumoured outbreaks but they were monitoring it carefully.

They were almost halfway to their destination now and were finding themselves in traffic that was getting heavier but was still moving. Going home would be a problem if social media was showing that this virus had spread.

"This is a testament to the great British mentality. It's this mentality that got us through The Blitz," Bobby said.

"Once people start seeing infected people coming their way it'll be back to the 'pull the ladder up jack and fuck everyone else' bullshit society is riddled with," Claire said.

Bobby smiled at her, "That's the sorta thing I'd come out with, I'm so proud of you." It wasn't just the words, it was how she said them. They sounded like something a Brit would say.

"Fuck off."

"After all these years my cynicism has rubbed off on you."

"If you don't shut up I'll never rub anything of yours again."

"Shutting right the fuck up." He winked and looked back to the road. "Look at that, there's that Merc that flew past us like a bat outta hell."

Claire looked up from her phone. "He got far."

Bobby was about to reply when a tipper truck sliced through the barrier from the other side of the motorway a hundred yards ahead of them, taking six cars out as it cut through the lanes. Bobby slammed his foot on the brake as hard as he could as cars ahead of them crashed into the ones that had been hit by the tipper lorry.

The Range Rover stopped just shy of the car in front that had hit a small van in front of them. Bobby had an eye shut, face fixed in a wince as he waited for something to rear-end them. Claire had her hands on the dash board, which was really dumb because if they'd crashed the airbags would have obliterated her arms. Both of them were breathing hard. Bobby took one of Claire's hands and gave it a kiss and then rubbed his shoulder where the seatbelt had kicked in.

The tipper truck had plowed through into a field and still hadn't stopped, leaving a scene of chaos behind it.

"Holy shit!" Claire said.

"That was closer than I'd have liked. Any closer and we'd have been in the back of that van too," Bobby said as people began getting out of their cars. "Are you okay?"

"Yeah, I might need to change my knickers though. Jesus, how didn't we get hit?" Claire said as she surveyed the devastation around them. "Seriously, we're the only thing not to. Are you okay?"

Bobby nodded and gave her a reassuring smile. He knew that had scared her because her accent had come through without any thought of suppressing it. "That was far too fucking close, never been that close without actually having a smack before."

Claire nodded, but Bobby didn't think she really knew why she was nodding. Not much scared her, but this had done. Being in a car where someone had deliberately crashed it to demonstrate their control over you had a lasting effect. He took her hand and kissed it, releasing some of the tension from her like his touch tended to do.

Bobby glanced to the clock on the Range Rover's dash. "We can't get held up here." Around them people were getting out of their vehicles and checking the damage that had been done or going to the aid of people who hadn't moved. "The fact that nothing's caught fire yet is pure luck, I don't want to be here when that luck runs out."

"What are you thinking? Not much of a clear route up ahead. There's a few cars blocking the hard shoulder." Claire had her accent hidden again.

They were surrounded by vehicles and it would take some weaving to get through the jam of cars around them, and that would be if they were lucky enough to be able to squeeze the big vehicle through.

"There's a gap on the inside of us just there that'll be tight but if slip through then there's another gap there and that'll take us onto the hard shoulder there where it's clear. Then we can get past the crash and the cars that have stopped the other side of the lorry's wake and we'll be clear."

"Don't run anyone over."

They got shouted at as they weaved their way through the traffic, those who'd got out of their vehicles having to move aside as the Range Rover approached. One man especially took offence to what they were doing and he and a woman were very vocal in voicing their anger. It came to a point where the man stood in front of the SUV.

"Ugh, we ain't got time for this."

"I'd say be gentle but he's big," Claire said as Bobby got out of the Range Rover. She watched as the man stormed around the front of the vehicle, hurling abuse at Bobby. He didn't say a word but did a flying roundhouse kick that left the guy on the ground trying to figure out what had hit him. The woman screamed at Bobby. Claire sighed and got out.

"You gonna do that to me? Huh? You gonna hit a woman?"

Bobby stood in front of the woman as she yelled at him. He'd defend himself if he had to but he wouldn't just hit her. Claire had no problems though. She grabbed the woman's shoulder and head butted her.

They dragged the man and woman out of the way and got back in the Range Rover and were pulling off as the shocked observers began filming their departure.

"Fucking ignorant arseholes. Ignoring the fact we weren't directly affected by the accident and there's plenty of other witnesses, there's also a virus spreading. For all we know that's why the lorry went through the barrier. You okay?"

Claire was looking at her forehead in the mirror on the back of the sun visor. "Yeah, she had hard head. Mouthy bitch. We've just got to hope they don't call the police on us. I'm sure a few of them will."

"We'll be clear by then. When the police get there they'll have all that mess to deal with. We're a minor footnote."

"Is it worth turning off?"

Bobby thought for a minute, "No, I think stick with the plan. Another hour and we're all but there. In an hour's time it'll still be chaos back there."

Claire nodded. "Maybe an alternate route home though, that'll back up both carriageways for hours."

"Good idea, have a look and see what you think will be best and check in with Chuck." They both knew the roads of the British mainland well but they'd both learnt that it was always best to check routes for changes or roadworks, or closures. The virus added to the equation, but Bobby didn't think it'll affect them too much.

Eight

The rest of the journey was quiet until they got into the outskirts of Birmingham and had to take a detour as the road to Edgebaston was shut. They followed diversions and then an alternate route that Claire had worked out.

It was approaching the midnight deadline but they'd still be there on time unless they hit another hold up, which they did.

They turned onto a street where there was a coach parked on the road, blocking one lane. A number of cars with their doors open were scattered around it. A single figure stumbled into view from behind a van. Illuminated by the SUVs headlights the person stopped moving and turned slowly to face them. Its head twitched and it shuffled towards them.

"Is that a zombie?" Claire said, her English accent fully slipped as her brain tried to process what she was looking at.

Bobby was pretty sure he'd have let his accent slip if he was hiding one. "Yeah."

There had been a lot of talk about how this virus affected people, but this word was the only way that

Bobby thought described what they were looking at accurately.

The zombie had an arm hanging limply, like it had been dislocated. Blood smeared its face and soaked its clothes.

Bobby leaned forward, "It's eyes look cloudy,"

More figures appeared from behind the parked vehicles. All blood covered like the first one. The mouth of one was chewing a red mess, a line of crimson spittle dangling from its lips. Another had its intestines hanging between its legs. A child moved through the twenty or so zombies. It wasn't running, but it moved quicker than the larger ones around it. Its eyes were glazed over like the others. Behind it was an old man who still had a crutch stuck to its arm that was being dragged along behind it. The glasses it wore were askew on its face.

The child was just ten feet from them now.

"Fuck fuck fuck, what are we going to do? There's fucking zombies out there!"

"Okay, um, let's double back and find another route." Bobby's hands shook as he slid the vehicle into reverse. He closed his eyes and willed his hands to still and be as steady as they had done for his entire life. He opened his eyes and looked back to begin reversing and saw more zombies.

"We're fucked." Claire pointed at the screen in the centre console and the image from the reverse camera.

In the darkness Bobby could see another half a dozen zombies. The child banged a hand against the front of the SUV, others joined it and began surrounding them. Bobby double checked that the doors were locked.

"Tell me you got it?" Claire said moving closer to the centre of the vehicle.

"Yeah, but if I go out there I'm dead." Bobby looked at the windows, "They're double glazed or reinforced, they ain't getting in."

Claire was almost on Bobby's lap now. "That's not stopping them from trying," With the car surrounded the zombies were beating on every surface they could reach, the white paint work showing the bloodied handprints easily. The windows were receiving the same treatment.

"What are we going to do?"

Bobby squeezed the steering wheel until his knuckles turned white."Fuck it! Back in your seat." Bobby gave Claire a little help getting seated and put the SUV into drive and took his foot off the brake. They drove forward slowly. The zombies didn't move out of the way so Bobby put a touch of pressure on the accelerator and made the vehicle push its way through them.

"Really? We're really doing this?" Claire said.

"We are, they ain't moving fast except for that kid. We get clear and to the drop off point and then we're gone. I'm not being fucked about any more. We go forward. We've got better visibility and won't have to find another route. Text Chuck, let him know what's happening."

Bobby pressed the pedal a little harder and the Range Rover responded. Now it wasn't pushing the zombies, it was running them down and rocking as it went over the undead. Claire was happy she couldn't hear their bones breaking under the wheels, she shut her eyes though. She was grateful there were only a few and with a final thud they were through them and Bobby put his foot down and drove the last mile to the drop off point.

All the shit she'd been through in her life hadn't quite prepared her for this, but it had helped.

Nine

They parked the SUV on a side street near the Edgbaston cricket ground and both looked around at the quiet road before getting out of the vehicle.

This was the most dangerous part, and the only time when Bobby had the pistol in a holster on his hip, but hidden under his jacket. Throughout the journey it had been in his bag in the vehicle but close to hand. He'd never had to use it but that didn't mean he wouldn't.

Bobby lit a cigarette as Claire rubbed down the surfaces of the Range Rover's interior. They wore gloves but Claire had taken those off at times while using her phone and tablet, and it never hurt to be double sure.

Bobby didn't smoke, had never done with the exception of these moments. Someone standing outside of a car looked odd. Someone standing outside a car while smoking didn't look odd. He hated the taste, and couldn't wait to get some mouthwash and swirl it around his mouth but it served a good purpose.

"It's good in there," Claire said with their bags.

Just as Bobby was going to reply, car doors opened and two men got out and started cheering and whooping. Bobby put his hand on the pistol as the two men walked up to them, bouncing off each other, looking like they'd just scored the winning goal in the cup. Then Bobby recognised them.

"Danny Wright and Ben Drake? What the fuck are you two doing here?"

"Who are they?" Claire asked.

"They play for Birmingham."

"Cheers for getting the Range here," Drake said as Wright went to the tailgate and opened it.

"We did it, dude!" Wright said.

"Fucking hell that was awesome!" The 'body 'in the boot said as he fought free of the bag he'd been in. He high-fived Wright. "I really need to piss!" He turned and pissed on the wheel of the SUV.

"Scott Tudor." Bobby shook his head. "Plays for the Hammers but at Birmingham on loan." He said to Claire, who was fuming.

"What the fuck! Was this some fucking game to you?"

The three men turned to look at Bobby and Claire.

Tudor stepped forward. "Well, I bet these two that I could go out and not get pissed on a Saturday night, and lost the bet. The forfeit was to be thrown in the boot of a car and driven for a few hours. Neither of these two pricks wanted to do the driving so we thought let's see how far we can go with it, and got you two."

"Just how did you get us?" Bobby said.

"Well, Benny here knows a guy who gets us some gear, you know? And he knows a guy who knows a guy."

"We get it," Bobby said. "Didn't you think it a good idea to knock it on the head when the mother fucking zombie apocalypse began?"

"We thought about it, but fuck it! It made it more fun," Wright said.

"Yeah, dude. I haven't been that fucking wired for years. Like it must be what war is like, living on the edge of death. I'm seriously banging some little groupie tonight." Tudor and Wright chest bumped each other.

"Pay us," Claire said.

"Yeah, you guys did a bang up job though. I won't even deduct the cost of the damage to the Range."

Tudor pulled a mobile phone from his pocket. "You sounded like you enjoyed your blowjob by the way."

Bobby and Claire shared a glance. Claire's phone pinged but she didn't check it. Bobby saw the flashbacks hitting her. Bobby had met her after she'd escaped her devil who'd trafficked her to Belgium, and then the UK. She'd managed to escape him and his circle of demons and was working in a Chinese takeaway, she was off the books and renting essentially a cupboard from a weasel who was creeping on her.

They'd met, and she'd been hesitant but Bobby had kept trying, careful not to overstep and slowly she started to trust him, finally revealing her past. He helped her get a new identity, putting Svetlana in the grave, and giving birth to Claire. He knew the right people and even in this day and age it was easy when you knew the right people and had deep pockets. Her devil had shown up to collect her body, but there wasn't one, and he was told she'd already been cremated. Bobby had put a bullet in the back of his head two days later while he was getting a massage.

It had taken her a long time for their relationship to become physical, but he'd let her set their pace and had helped her discover that sex was something to be enjoyed. Now, she owned her sexuality, but there was still things that triggered her. Being watched was one of them.

"It's done." Claire said so softy he barely heard her

"Good," Bobby said, and punched Ben Drake, head-butted Danny Wright, and slammed Scott Tudor's head into the bonnet of the Range Rover.

"What the fuck?" Drake said.

"You wanna play little rich prick games, go and get a fucking reality show. You fuck with us and you are fucking lucky to walk away." He grabbed Tudor's trademark long blond hair, pulled a butterfly knife from his pocket and cut the golden locks away.

"Do you think this is a fucking joke now? You think because you have money you can do whatever the fuck you want? You think it gives you power?" Bobby pulled the pistol from the holster. "This will take everything you have away in less than a heartbeat. I'm not some fucking star struck cunt, I get paid to do serious shit and no questions asked. I could pull this fucking trigger, blow your fucking brains out and no fucker will pull me on it." He pushed the barrel of the gun harder against Tudor's forehead. "You've put me and my partner in danger because you thought it would be funny. I'm not a fucking pawn in your game."

Bobby fired three quick shots, one in a leg of each of these men. "You try and contact me again, I'll blow the back of your fucking head out while you sit on the throne taking a shit. You tell anybody about this I'll kill your fucking families. You understand?"

The three men took a little more encouragement to show they understood. Tudor pissed himself while Bobby had the gun pressed to his ear.

Ten

They left the three footballers where they had fallen. If they survived the night, and the world didn't end, their careers would likely be over. No one hurt him or Claire. Wary of the threat of the zombies they moved quickly and without talking three roads over to where a non-descript Mondeo was parked. The man in the drivers seat got out of it.

"All sorted?" Chuck said.

"I'll explain on the way home," Bobby said. Chuck was one of the few people who Bobby trusted, an old friend from his Iraq days. Chuck wasn't in this life anymore, only when Bobby and Claire needed another driver.

"Okay, you think we've got anything to worry about getting home?"

"After that journey I hope not, but after that journey I know it's going to be a bitch." Bobby looked around at the quiet street. He had a feeling they needed to get out of the built up areas and back to their village quickly.

Straight Home

"I love having a cinema to ourselves. No idiots talking throughout the film, priceless" Stefan said as the credits rolled.

"I hear that." PJ turned his phone on. Stefan did the same.

Both of their phones erupted with texts, missed calls, and voice mails.

PJ read the text messages quickly. "Holy shit mate, there's people saying that plague stuff has spread, you know that shit in Prague. All over the place, including London," Stefan said.

"Seriously?"

PJ showed him his phone.

"Oh shit."

PJ turned back to his phone as it rang. "Hey Dad."

"What's the fucking point in having a mobile phone if you turn the thing off! We've been trying to call you for hours. Check your phone and you'll see all the shit that is kicking off out there. Get here now. Stefan too! It's too dangerous to get him back to Sittingbourne. Get in that bloody orange sports car of yours and get home. No dicking about. Straight home!"

"I think you're crashing at mine."

There was a scream outside of screen nine.

"That sounded very fucking real dude," PJ said.

Stefan called his folks quickly, and got yelled at for turning his phone off before telling them he'd be staying at PJ's. They made their way to the doors. Both sets were shut and they opened the first one slowly to see the small space between the two sets of doors empty. The outer doors that lead into the lobby of the cinema were shut.

"Maybe a later screening wasn't the best idea," PJ said.

"You okayed the time."

"I'm not having a pop, just saying."

Stepping out the next set of double doors they peered towards the lobby but didn't see anyone, although the concessions racks had been knocked over and popcorn was scattered across the floor.

"You see anything, mate?"

"We're looking at the same thing," PJ said.

They both edged out slowly.

"You got any weapons in your car?" Stefan said.

"Yeah, I've got a couple M16's, some Desert Eagle's, oh and thank fuck I remembered to pack my rocket propelled grenade."

"Dick."

"I've got a hockey stick and lever bar in the boot," PJ said.

"Sweet, I need to pee first."

"Really? You want to go into an enclosed space with only one way in and out?"

Stefan held a hand up. "Point. I'll pee outside."

The lobby was clear of people, but not blood, which there was a lot of. Three of the glass doors were shattered and Frankie's was on fire.

"Shit, I was meant to take Mia there tomorrow," PJ said.

"Just go the Maidstone one."

PJ laughed, "I think we might have bigger issues to deal with to be honest."

They jogged out of the cinema building and into what looked like the set from a Hollywood movie. There were bodies lying around everywhere, some of which were in pieces. There were cars on fire in the car park to their right. Screams were coming from their left.

"God, I hope my car's still in one piece," PJ said.

"You ready to run for it?"

Stefan shook his legs out. "I was born ready."

"Really? You couldn't have chosen a better time than that for that line?"

"We might not get another chance. Just because we've got an apocalypse out here doesn't mean we'll get a better chance for that line."

PJ sighed, "Let's go."

They bolted, and PJ tripped over a curb and went sprawling across gravel.

"Come on, mate. Mia'll kick my arse if you get eaten by a horde of zombies."

"Not my fault some twat put a curb there."

PJ's orange Ford Focus ST was right where he'd left it, and in one piece.

"Get in, I'll get the weapons."

A moment after Stefan had got in PJ threw a hockey stick and a lever bar on the back seat. The lever bar was almost as long as the hockey stick.

"What do you need that for?"

"In case I need to get a wheel off."

"It's huge," Stefan said.

"That's what she said."

"And you give me shit for my one liners."

"But mine was funny."

"You keep telling yourself that. Can we go now? And are you sure your place is gonna be better?"

"It's gotta be. It's a bit more isolated, so less people who'll become zombies and it's got a big fucking wall around it," PJ said.

Stefan looked bemused. "Yeah mate, that works. You got beer at yours? Or just that pansy alco-pop shite?"

"There's nothing wrong with being a lightweight, and a proud lightweight at that."

"You keep telling yourself that, especially when your missus is drinking you under the table."

PJ flipped him off and pulled out of the parking spot and swerved around the cars that had been abandoned or had crashed.

"If it wasn't for the blood and distant screams you'd never know something was wrong by how these cars are parked," Stefan said.

"I hear that. People can't park down here for shit at the best of times. Like that Audi. Is that dumped there because of whatever's happening or has the owner just parked it in four spaces because he's a prick?"

"My money's on him, or her, being a prick," Stefan said.

They drove through Medway Park, swerving around a couple of cars, and a body that was missing a head but had a long blood smear on the tarmac where a car had smooshed the head into the road. Maccy D's drive through was bumper to bumper, literally. One car had hit another and it had dominoed through all the cars there. Like ghouls they drove past slowly and took in all the blood splatter in and on the cars. One of the service windows had an employee hanging from it. They were both looking at the dead body when something bounced off the car's bonnet.

"Did I just hit someone? Or was it a zombie?"

"I don't know, you're driving."

"Fuck." PJ checked his mirror and backed up until they could see the body on the road ahead of them lit by the cars headlights. It writhed and was dragging itself towards them, eyes a dirty creamy colour and jaw hanging like it had been dislocated.

"Is that a zombie?"

"Yeah, thank fuck for that," PJ said and began to pull away.

"Wait, shouldn't we deal with it?"

"Really? You wanna go out there?"

"I don't want to but don't you think we should, like, pop our zombie killing cherries?"

PJ wanted to take this seriously and be sensible in a dangerous situation, but he also wanted to kill a zombie. "Yeah okay, but don't do anything stupid."

"Speaks the man who slept with Bianca Adams."

"Really? You're bringing Bianca Adams up now? How was I supposed to know she was a nutter? And if everyone knew she was a nutter why didn't none of you tell me?"

"It's not like you texted anyone to say, 'hey I've just pulled this bird called Bianca Adams. The first we knew about it was when she was posting on FB that, and I quote 'If anyone goes near PJ Watson I'll fuck them up 'end quote."

PJ looked at his best friend, "Yeah okay."

The zombie slammed a hand onto the bonnet and both men turned back to the undead in front of them.

"Okay, who gets the first whack?"

"My idea, so I get the first hit. Can I use the hockey stick?"

"No, that's my lucky hockey stick, only I'm using it."

"Alright, touchy. Just cause I called dibs on the first zombie."

They got out the car, while leaving it running and approached the zombie. PJ kept a keen eye out as he didn't want any other survivors to sneak up on him, and he didn't want any wankers to nick his car.

"Both his legs are broken. Look at that jaw, I'm not sure he could bite us if he wanted to."

"Mate, he's a zombie, of course he wants to fucking bite and likely eat us until his guts burst from his

30

abdomen."

"Are your guts in the abdomen? Or is it called something else?"

PJ shrugged, "Are you gonna hit it or not? It's coming your way."

"Yeah," Stefan took a breath and swung the metal bar and whacked the zombie on the back of its head. The crack was sickening but the zombie slumped to the ground and didn't get back up again.

"Holy shit that was not as hard as I thought it was gonna be. Shit, I needed to pee."

"Don't you now? Did you have an accident?"

"No." He checked his crotch. "No, I'm good. Keep your eye out, I don't want to die with my dick in my hand."

Stefan went over to a nearby bush, undid his jeans and relieved himself. "Damn I needed that, oh shit."

"What?"

"There's a fucking set of legs here, like just a set of legs."

PJ joined him. "Where the hell's the rest of him, or her?"

'Oh come on, it's gotta be a dude, no woman in their right mind would wear something that hideous," Stefan said.

"Gender has nothing to do with dress sense,"

"I don't think you have any grounds to comment on anyone's fashion sense."

PJ looked at his Doc Martens, black jeans, and hoodie that had angel wings on the back. "Speaks the man who cosplays as a geography teacher."

"Arsehole." Stefan laughed. "Seriously though, where's the rest of it? Do you think it was, like, sliced in two and the other half is dragging itself around without anything from the waist down?"

"That's gotta suck, like do zombies have to shit? I mean they eat brains and everything else, but what happens to the flesh they consume? Surely there's some waste, it can't all be digested."

"I dunno, but there's a blood smear going towards the Premier Inn. Shall we go and see where it goes? It looks quite fresh."

"I'm not too sure I want to be going into a building like that. Tackling them in the open is one thing but not in a confined space. Not right away, anyway."

"Probably a good idea."

"Come on," PJ said, assessing the dent on his bonnet from where the zombie bounced off it.

Once they'd pulled up to the roundabout they saw more chaos. Notably a Royal Mail truck on its side.

"I hope my bank statement isn't in that lot," PJ said of the letters that were flying on the wind.

"Ain't you got a banking app?"

"I forgot me password thingy. It needed at least one upper case letter, a number, had to be at least eight characters and have the pubic hair from an orangutan."

"At least it's not blocking the motorway," Stefan said.

"You know what this means?"

"No post for a couple of days?"

"No, the police will be pre-occupied with the undead and not with people who may be pushing the speed limit a little bit. Wanna see how quickly we can get to Bluebell Hill and back?"

Stefan smiled. "I'll time it, from when we get on the slip road?"

"Yeah, let's go!" PJ slipped the car into first gear and shot away from the roundabout.

This stretch of road was a little windy and had walls of brick and rock either side, so although he drove fast he didn't floor it until the road opened up as they crossed the bridge that took then across the M2. Here it was surprisingly clear, aside from a pushbike that was on the pavement on their left. The next roundabout was clear as they went right, down towards the slip roads. They passed the London bound one faster than PJ had ever navigated this stretch of road and did the same at the next roundabout as he took it to the right and onto the coast bound slip road, red-lining the rev counter before changing gear.

"And we're ticking!" Stefan said with iPhone in hand and the timer going as PJ pushed the Focus harder than he'd ever done before.

On the M2 there was little traffic, a few red taillights some miles ahead of them and a headlight in the distance behind them. There was more traffic on the London bound carriageway but they'd deal with that once they were on the return leg of the journey.

The car passed one hundred miles per hour and then one ten as PJ overtook a lorry. Ahead there were now more vehicles but still not as many as he'd have expected for nigh on midnight on a weeknight.

PJ glanced in his mirror, the fear of pursuing blue lights growing as the lorry they had just passed swerved and went up the embankment. "Holy shit that lorry's just gone up off the road."

"Where?" Stefan turned in his seat. "Fuuuuuck, it's gone over."

PJ looked in his mirrors and saw the lorry on its side, and only just saw a car ahead of him swerve into the barrier and spin off across all four lanes.

"Maybe this wasn't such a good idea," Stefan said.

"I hear that, let's get to Bluebell, spin around and get back to mine and no more fucking about."

"Deal, shit," Stefan said. "I hadn't realised how

foggy it had got."

"Bluebell Hill dude, it's known for three things: The Bride, the fog, and the fucking traffic."

"Ah, it's not the bride who died. It was a bridesmaid. The bride died like a week later or something."

"Huh, I always thought it was a bride who died."

"Me too, but I was chatting to Kayleigh at work about it the other day and she said it was the bridesmaid. Obviously I Googled it when I got back to me desk to make sure she wasn't having a laugh but yeah."

"Well, let's not become another pair of ghosts on this road," PJ said and put his fog lights on.

"Aaaand we've driven into Silent Hill." Stefan said as the fog got noticeably thicker as they came off the motorway.

"Why would you bring that up now? That's like when you're on a date and the first thing you do is mention your ex."

"We'll be alright, just don't stop."

PJ pointed to the top of the slip road, the notorious Bluebell Hill roundabout where the traffic lights were changing from green, to amber and then to red. "What about those?"

"Shite. I'd say drive straight through but it's Bluebell Hill."

"Exactly, especially seeing how thick this fog is. I can't see shit."

"Lock the doors?"

With the doors locked PJ pulled the Focus up to the line and waited for the lights to turn green. "You keep an eye out, I'll watch the lights."

"On it!"

PJ had the clutch at biting point and would be off the moment that light went to amber. He pulled off as soon as it did, and almost got taken out by someone in an Astra.

"Fucking light jumping areshole!" PJ yelled at the other driver who was already out of sight.

"See, you can be the most sensible driver in the world but then some twat in an Astra ruins your day," Stefan said.

"Prick," PJ said and pulled away, a little more cautiously as he eyed the road around him.

They had no other close shaves while on Bluebell Hill, although they saw a number of cars on fire down towards the Maidstone exit.

The London bound slip road onto the M2 from Bluebell Hill was clear until they were halfway down it. There was a police car on its roof with a zombified officer struggling to free itself from its seat belt.

"If we went and whacked it on the head does that still count as assaulting a police officer?" PJ said.

"If it does that one I hit at the cinema is assault then, or murder."

"That's self-defence though."

"It would have been if we hadn't run it over first," Stefan said, "Fuck it. We just won't tell anyone."

"I'm sure it'll be considered exceptional circumstances."

"There's more blue lights up ahead, mate." Stefan pointed to the dull flashing lights of emergency services vehicles ahead of them. "Get over to the left, looks like it's over on the outer lanes."

PJ did this, then had to swerve to stop from running over a body that was in the road. "I'll be glad once we're out of this fog."

They had to slow down to ten miles per hour as they got to the blue lights. There were vehicles everywhere. Four of which were emergency services: Three police cars and an ambulance. Each with doors open. The civilian vehicles were the same. Two lorries, one of which was on its side blocking all but the inside lane and the hard shoulder. There was an eighth car under the lorry's trailer and three other cars that had collided with the lorry. Almost all of the cars had at least one of their doors open. As PJ and Stefan got closer they saw what looked like blood splashed everywhere. It was hard to tell in the dark of night and thick fog, and there was no way PJ was going to stop to investigate.

As they passed the back of the ambulance they looked into it. It was lit with a harsh white light that left no question of the blood that covered its interior.

"Okay, what worries me is where are all the people that were here? There's like a dozen vehicles here and just that one body back there."

"I don't wanna know. If we'd been able to see this from the other carriageway then I would have turned around and gone on the wrong side of the road." PJ pulled away from the back of the ambulance and weaved the car around the bigger pieces of debris and anything that may burst a tyre.

"Hopefully the fog will ease off soon, it's never this bad. Okay Bluebell Hill often has it but how often does it spread this far?"

"Not often, but I'm taking nothing for granted tonight." PJ drove on the hard shoulder as he avoided a motorbike.

"That's where the zombies are," Stefan said as the cars lights lit up a couple of zombies that were dragging themselves along the road in front of them.

"That one had to be the biker, we ain't giving him a blunt trauma to the head."

"Unless it's a cheap helmet."

The biker was right ahead of them and was pulling

itself along the road with one arm. The other was missing, and its legs were lifeless as it dragged itself towards an unknown goal.

"Can you see anything on that side of the road, I'm gonna have to get real close to that barrier."

"It looks clear, just keep it nice and easy."

The zombie's good arm was on the other side to which they passed but PJ saw it turn its head as they got closer. It started to turn and reached out so PJ put his foot down a little and got past the zombie as quickly as he felt comfortable going. He still heard a thud off the back door as they passed.

"You know I mentioned Silent Hill earlier?"

PJ looked ahead and saw the second zombie had dragged itself around and was crawling their way, and a dozen or more others were slowly emerging from the thick fog. All focused on the car that was illuminating them with its headlights. PJ doubled checked that the doors were locked.

"Fuck it, hold on," PJ said and drove. He didn't drive fast like they did in the movies. Knowing the way the night was going he'd hit a zombie and all his air bags would go off. Instead he drove around the largest cluster of the undead and navigated his way around the stragglers on the edges of the crowd.

They both winced as they drove over a lumpy object.

"Let's not wonder what that was," PJ said.

"Agreed," Stefan said.

"Hardly any reason to hold on though, mate. Not exactly breaking any land speed records here,"

"You're the one driving like a nun."

"Slow and steady wins the race. Well, until the roads clear and we're through this fog. What's being said online?"

Stefan grabbed his phone from the door pocket and began to scroll through the various social media platforms. "Looks like it's something to do with this Prague thingy that the papers have been on about for the last few days. Ha! A reporter had to be dragged out of a press conference with the PM after he called her out for not calling them zombies."

"You can't blame her though, it'll be like if vampires suddenly popped their heads out from the shadows and said 'hey we actually exist. 'Especially after only a few hours."

"I wonder what bullshit they'll come up with to explain this lot, and who's to blame for it all," Stefan said.

"I'm sure one side will blame the other side and vice versa. Or they'll just say its Covid having a fightback." PJ swerved around the last zombie he could see and pushed the accelerator down a touch more. "Looks like it's clearing." They picked up more speed as the fog thinned and finally cleared as they were crossing the Medway Bridge.

It wasn't a long drive to the Shorne, Higham, and Cobham turn off but he took it slowly. Not once did PJ push the car above sixty miles per hour. The road was empty, as was the slip road. There were no other cars on the road but once they were on Halfpence Lane they saw three zombies.

"How bad do you think it really is?" Stefan said, but PJ couldn't answer as a car gave a blast from its horn and flew past them, sending a zombie over its bonnet.

"He's in a hurry." PJ drove on.

"They're calling a state of emergency and ordering everyone to stay in their homes or where you are until further notice."

"Not far to go now," PJ said, "Shit, we've just got to

get through Cobham."

"Fuck, we shoulda gone the other way, come off at Gravesend East. Turn around?"

"No, we're best part of the way there now. You know what Cobham is like, everyone's probably in bed already and we'll sail through."

They didn't.

"Well shit, I guess we've got to get back on the motorway," PJ said. The car that had raced by them was wedged between the buildings on this old narrow street with the driver hanging out of the windscreen. PJ put the car in reverse. The parking sensors gave a continuous bleep, PJ looked at the screen in the centre consul and saw a zombie there. "Motherfuckers are everywhere."

"How close is that? Like, it's in the red lines and sensors are going batty."

"Very close, I'm gonna have to nudge it outta the way." The car jerked backwards and the zombie went flying.

"Christ, I thought you said you were gonna nudge it."

"I did, it was just a bit more of a nudge than I was planning."

After a quick three point turn they were out of Cobham village and heading back to the A2. Two cars went by them at speed as they passed the car park for Ashenbank Wood. There was a third car but that was on its roof on the roundabout with its driver having been dragged out and was being eaten by two zombies.

"That's got to be a cramper on your day," Stefan said.

"Let's not have our day end like that."

They got onto the A2 and saw another clear stretch of road. A few cars passed them on the coast bound carriageway and PJ could see a couple of taillights up ahead but they were beyond the Gravesend East exit. PJ pushed the car hard for those few hundred metres and came off gently onto Jeskyns Road, where they saw a couple of the dead wandering along the road but passed them before they'd had the chance to stumble into the car's path. PJ turned onto Sole Street and immediately turned right into their old farm yard. His dad had bought it ten years ago and converted it all into housing for the family. There was also a big gate that they could shut and keep any one, dead or alive, out with. It started opening as they approached and shut quickly once they were in. His brother and dad were there, with his mum and grandmother watching on.

"What took you so long?"

"Hey dad, good to see you too."

PJ looked around the old farmyard. "So, what now?"

Farmers Vs. Zombies

One

The combine harvester wouldn't start, and had been resisting for the last two hours. Josh Holloway swore under his breath, when he'd rather be cussing at the top of his throat and slamming the three foot long wrench against the old piece of shit. But his two kids were in the farmyard. His fifteen year old daughter wouldn't be bothered, but his seven year old son was liable to repeat such outbursts at school for the entertainment of his classmates.

It had been a good bit of kit, but he was looking forward to taking delivery of his new Klass before the next harvest, and although the last harvest was done and this one could finally be retired they couldn't leave it where it was parked in the yard.

Sonny, who'd come to work for him at the start of the harvest, and he'd kept on, had wanted to tinker with it over the winter. Josh was quite happy for him to do that in his spare time, no one had come forward to buy it and the dealer hadn't offered him a decent price on it. It could go inside until the new one arrived, but they had to get it running to get it inside. How it had lasted the harvest Josh didn't know, which also explained why he'd had a low offer on the trade in.

Sonny was still young, but had settled in well. He'd be a good replacement for Pete who would be retiring in the next couple of years. He wasn't a farm boy but had gone to Agriculture College and learnt that way. He'd also worked the land during harvest and other breaks from school.

Josh was a farm lad to the core. His family owned a lot of the local land and had farmed it for generations.

That hadn't stopped Josh doing the backpacking across America thing for a couple of years. Working on farms out there to pay his way. He'd come back and things had changed. The other farmers in the area had gone against his family because his dad, Frank, wouldn't sell his land to three other land owners. They'd been trying to convince him to do so about the time Josh had let his family know he'd be coming home and couldn't wait to get stuck in. Neither of Josh's sisters had been interested and apparently his father had got it into his head that Josh wasn't either, despite what he'd said before leaving. It wasn't 'til he'd come home that his father had realised that Josh had just wanted to spend a couple of years travelling. Although he hadn't expected to come home with the woman he'd end up marrying.

This resulted in few of the local farmers not having anything to do with them because although no promises had been made, they thought they'd have the land to divide up between them when Frank retired. Josh's land was almost what the other three major farmers in the area had combined. He could live with it though, because he had so much land it meant that few people outside the village really took sides. Holloway Farm produced far too much for wholesalers to get involved.

"No joy?" Sonny said.

Josh liked Sonny. He wasn't put off by the lad's six inch long goatee, long hair, or the piercings and amount of tattoos he had. Josh had initially thought 'goth 'when he'd first met him but Sonny had said that he wasn't quite there, more of a metal head horror nut. For a twenty-four year old he had his head screwed on and Josh liked that about him.

"No, I think the technical term is 'fucked'." Josh looked over his shoulder to make sure his kids were out of ear shot.

"Has it got fuel?"

"Don't be a smart arse."

Sonny smiled as he climbed into the cab. "Let me give it a go."

"Arsehole," Josh said as the harvester came to life. "There's a special place in hell for twats like you."

"People keep saying that to me."

Josh flipped him off. "Twat, straight into the shed."

Sonny smiled, "Really?"

"There's nothing that you can damage, except the building itself. So be careful."

"Sweet, cheers boss."

Two

Madeline Holloway had the news on as she cooked dinner. Tonight she was doing a curry that had been in the slow cooker most of the day and smelt amazing. Josh was in the shower and the kids were in the living room playing Mario Kart, loudly. Carrie had come along without much effort, but it had taken a long time for her get pregnant with Alec. They'd tried and tried, had a couple of false alarms but until Alec had come along they'd had a frustrating time of trying to conceive. They hadn't given up, but she thought if it had been another year and nothing then that conversation would have begun. Both her and Josh had been a little worried about the age gap, but Carrie doted on her little brother and Alec looked up to her.

Madeline was somewhat of a news junkie and had BBC News 24 on and was watching an article about a virus that had broken out in Prague which had people dropping dead on the streets and the city was now in quarantine. It was making Covid look like a puny cold.

She'd gone to Prague while on holiday with her parents when she'd been sixteen and had enjoyed the city and felt for them, but wasn't ashamed to say she was glad it was over there and not closer to her and her family.

She measured rice out as footage of fire pits filled with the dead was shown. Great timing she thought; people sitting down to dinner loved to see that.

"This is the sort of thing that'll lead to the apocalypse."

"Mum, how long's dinner gonna be?" Carrie called out.

"Five minutes, so think about pausing that game and getting ready, please"

Three

Josh and Madeline lay in silence as the rain outside fell hard enough to hear it hitting their bedroom windows as they caught their breath. They'd been married seventeen years and that passion was still there. They were both thirty-eight, with Madeline being three months older than Josh. A few times the passion had diminished, but it had never lasted long. They'd had hard times, but they'd endured them.

They both looked out the window as a flash of lightning lit the sky, followed a few seconds afterwards by a clap of thunder.

"What do you think of all this stuff in Prague?" she asked him.

"It doesn't look good from the stuff they've showed us on the news. It feels like the Czech government is hiding something. All this being 'uncooperative 'talk doesn't bode well."

"Hmm, it's scary the government haven't stopped flights in and out, and if it's contagious why haven't they shut the borders? Didn't they learn anything from Covid? It looks like they've got their heads in the sand." Madeline had taken Covid seriously as soon as she'd heard about it. She started stockpiling but not panic buying. She'd buy a couple of bits extra each time they'd gone shopping so when the shit did hit the fan there was no panic in the Holloway house. "It's not like the Czech's either, well doesn't seem like them anyway."

"Politicians. As a rule they all like sticking their head in the sand."

"Still worrying though. What if, whatever it is, has got out? If it's really contagious then it could get here quickly."

"Let's not worry about a what if. Let's keep an eye on the news and all that and see what happens. If the apocalypse comes we've got plenty of food and the diesel tank is topped off." Josh said. "And we've got livestock we can always slaughter."

"I can just imagine Carrie getting stuck into butchering a cow,"

Josh laughed, "If she want's Ribeye she'll have to,"

Four

"Fuck it!"

Josh stopped in his tracks at the sudden outburst as he stepped into the main barn. It was only a hundred yards from his house and he carried two cups of tea.

"Mother fucking twatting spawn of Lucifer's rectal warts."

"You take cursing to a whole new level, Sonny."

Josh heard a thud and he couldn't decipher what the new string of expletives were as Sonny appeared from the guts of the combine rubbing his head. His long hair was tied into a pony tail and tucked down the back of his overalls, but Josh could see that he'd shaved the left side above his ear and had dyed some of it a fiery orange that stood out against his natural black.

"Nice," Josh said while pointing to his own head.

"You'd rock a bold red."

"Been there, done that."

"Seriously?"

"Yeah. When I was in LA I lived above a tattoo parlour for a while and ended with a red faux hawk."

"Please tell me there's pics?"

"Loads, scroll through my tagged ones on Facebook sometime."

"Nice, that where you got your ink?"

"Some of it, the rest I got in town. That's where I got the love for it though."

"I want to get me sleeve," Sonny was interrupted by the office phone ringing.

"Holloway Farm, hello? Really? Heavy breathing? And you're calling a farm? Twat." Josh hung up.

"People are weird, man."

They both looked at each and then ran as they heard a scream shooting across the farmyard. Josh's blood froze as he saw a ratty looking man trying to get into his house. He ran faster but was still a step behind the younger Sonny. The bloodied smears on the door pulled a little more pace out of him.

"Oi, arsehole, what the fuck do you think you're doing?" Josh yelled as he ran.

Slowly the person turned. He was missing its face.

"Fucking hell!"

"Shit," Sonny added, "Is that a zombie?"

"Don't be soft."

They both turned at a groan to their left. There were two more people coming their way, a man and a woman. The man looked whole but was only wearing a t-shirt and boxers and had a dirty complexion to his skin. The woman had a gaping hole where her throat should have been. Her clothes were bloodstained from the wound.

"I know them, they're staying at the pub. Just come back from Dresden or somewhere."

"Why are they here then?"

"Beats me."

The three people stumbled towards them.

"I don't give a shit who they are, what the fuck are they doing now?"

"Coming to eat our brains."

"Maddie, call the police."

Madeline appeared at the kitchen window with a phone in her hand. "Derrrr!"

"Fucking zombies on the farm and she's still being a smart arse. Did I really just say that?"

"Yep."

"If you three are fucking with us I'm gonna kick the shit out of you."

None of them reacted aside from their steady forward movement.

"This is fucked up," Sonny said as they both backed up.

Josh turned and looked around the farmyard. "Lead them into the small cattle yard. Where the chickens are gonna go."

"Yeah, good idea."

With a little coercion they got the three people into the small cattle yard. Most of the farmyard was as it had been for decades and all the cattle yards as they called them were enclosed by bricks. This structure served as the wall for two sides of the large farm yard with one side having the entrance and farm house. The fourth side had been open for years until Josh had built a new farm building that had all the heavy machinery in it.

"Now we've just got to get out," Sonny said.

"You go left, I'll go right and we shut the gate when we get out."

"Done."

Both men ran but hadn't needed to. The people were slow and sluggish and tripped over their own feet as they tried to go in two directions at once.

With a clank, the gate was shut, latched and locked. It was a solid wood one that Josh had built which wouldn't let a chicken escape, so he was confident these three wouldn't get out.

"That was easier than I thought." Sonny held his fist out.

Josh tapped his knuckles against Sonny's. "Boom."

"If you two are finished playing silly buggers, you need to check out the news."

Five

In the house Josh and Sonny watched the news in the kitchen with Madeline and Carrie. Alec was still in bed but would no doubt be up soon.

"This is gonna be like Shaun Of The Dead," Sonny said.

"I'm Shaun then."

"I'll be Ed, I can live with that," Sonny said.

"He dies," Josh said.

"Lasts longer than the twat with glasses."

"You two are unbelievable. It'll be more like Cockneys Vs. Zombies," Madeline said.

"And you call me immature," Carrie added. "And Ed doesn't die, he lives as a zombie in the shed playing video games."

"Joking aside, what are we going to do? I mean the news is talking about cities being quarantined like Prague is. They're trying to quarantine London but thousands are trying to get out. Manchester's the same."

"Mum, look at this." Carrie handed Madeline her iPad.

"Oh my god, people are attacking each other in the streets." She showed them footage of dozens of zombies attacking people.

"What did the police say?"

"I didn't get through, they must be getting a lot of calls."

"It's all over the place. It's got a hashtag, #ZombieBritain," Carrie said. "South East London and Kent, like here, are getting loads of these things in them."

"Outbreaks across the world," Sonny said looking at his own phone. "This all kicked off last night, how did we all miss it?"

"Well, we had family night last night," Josh said.

"We had an impromptu date night." Sonny smiled.

"How many people live in town?" Madeline said moving the conversation back to the topic at hand.

"Eighty thousand, I guess," Josh said.

"And what if they get it and come this way?"

"Do you want to leave?"

"No, I mean where would we go? We've already had three here. Is the rest of the village like that?"

"Guys, I've watched and read more zombie fiction than is probably good for one's mental health and I say stay here, for the moment at least. This place is pretty well walled in. All we need to do is plug a couple of gaps, the main entrance being the main one, but we got machinery we can use. There's one gated road in and out. Fuck it, personally I'd dig a fucking moat around the place," Sonny said.

"I can't believe we're having this conversation," Madeline said.

"Anything from the States?"

"No," Madeline said. "I've checked the news and there's nothing anywhere over there. I've checked locally as well and nothing's happened in Tulsa. My folks and sister will be in bed so I don't want to worry them unless I have to."

"Right, here's what we're gonna do: We're gonna block off the entrances, Sonny you go and get Tiffany and get back here, take one of the CB radios with you in case phones fuck up. Then we're going to dig a moat around the place and lock it down until it is all clear. We'll call my sisters and get them here."

"What about the curfew?"

"We'll chance it. Beth is the furthest away and that's only forty minutes."

"Can I take your Ranger though? My Jimny's been a little stroppy lately."

"Good idea, give your missus heads up and get her to pack what she needs."

"I'll call her now."

"No chances, get there and back again. Fuck anything else."

"Got it, boss."

"Grab one of those axes from the barn as you go. Just in case."

"What about the three in the yard?" Madeline said, "We can't just leave them there."

"We've got to deal with them," Josh said. "The news said to if you have to,"

"Dad, what do you mean?" Carrie said.

"If they get out."

Carrie held a hand up. "Like the fox that got caught in the chicken's fence?"

"Yeah."

"Okay, I don't need to see it though."

"Go make sure Alec doesn't look out his window."

"Okay, Mum."

Six

Josh stood and watched the hands of the people they'd trapped over the top of the six foot high wooden gate clawing to get out.

They both held axes, neither were ready for what they had to do. They hadn't had time to get their heads around it.

"You ready?"

"Nope."

"Me neither. Let's just do it."

Josh unbolted the door and pushed it, finding the people, the zombies easy to push back.

Josh took a slow breath as he looked at the eyes of the man who had been hitting the door. His eyes were not glazed over, the whites looked creamy and his iris ' looked odd. Like someone had bleached a little of their colour out.

Josh swallowed the bile that had climbed his throat and swung. The crack of the skull breaking as the axe hit it almost made Josh vomit. He had slaughtered a lot of different types of farm animal over his life, particularly in the US, but hadn't done any for years. He'd also shot foxes and the occasional dog that was terrorising his livestock. This wasn't that though, these had once been people, and that was a different prospect altogether

Another crack sounded and the second of the three slumped like the first had. Josh watched a moment as Sonny stood over it, and then the lad threw up. Seeing this Josh did the same. He didn't have time to wipe his mouth as the third one reached for him. Josh swung blindly, breaking an arm which didn't stop the thing that had once been a woman. He struck again with more composure and the axe got stuck in the zombie's head as it crumbled to the ground.

"Did you get any blood on you?" Sonny asked.

Josh looked himself up and down but didn't see anything. "I don't think so, have a look will yah?"

Sonny checked Josh over and then he checked Sonny.

"I hope we don't have to do that again," Sonny said.

"I second that,"

"What are we going to do with them?"

"Go get Tiffany, I'll sort them out."

Seven

As Sonny drove down the lane Josh went over to his folk's cottage, his dad came out the door with a double-barrelled shotgun ready.

"Dad, Really?"

"The radio said zombies."

"It also said to hit them on the head."

"If I blow their bloody heads off it'll have the same effect."

He had him there.

"Ah, but then you'll splatter their brains everywhere and if it gets on someone it could infect them."

"Don't be bloody soft! I'd never shoot when someone may get caught in the shot who I wasn't aiming for."

"Okay, whatever. We're moving everyone into the farmhouse. It's big enough for everyone, it's also pretty well walled in. So get Mum and grab whatever you need."

"Why? We're good here."

"Strength in numbers, Dad. We get everyone in the main farmhouse we can secure the yard easily. Right now those things could just stroll along and surround the cottages."

"I suppose you're right,"

Eight

Once they'd got his mother, Monique, who wasn't too good on her feet anymore, into the main farmhouse, Josh and his Dad, who was in good shape for a man nearing his seventy-fourth birthday, went to the small cattle yard and pulled the bodies of the three zombies out.

"Jesus fucking Christ that's some nasty shit," Frank said.

"I know, right."

"What's your plan now?"

"I was gonna pop them in the loader and take them down the road and burn them. I don't really want any scavengers getting hold of them."

"Good, while you're doing that I'll get the gaps in the yard walls plugged up."

"Cheers, Dad. Everything has gates, and aside from the main one they're all closed and locked. I was thinking we put bulk trailers against the big gates but knock them on their sides. That way nothing will get under them."

"What did you want to put across the main gate?"

"I was thinking the harvester. We know it barely fits through with the header on, so we drive it up to the gate and just leave it there. Then we back it up if we need to get in and out."

His old man thought this out for a moment, scratching his chin as he always did when he was trying to think something out. "That should work. I'm glad we never tore down that side of the yard now." Frank nodded at the old cattle barns.

"Same here, Sonny reckons we should dig a moat around the place as well. Leaving only the track clear. I'm a bit worried about the cattle and sheep out in the fields. The pigs are alright where they are for the moment I think, and the chickens are still in the little run in the garden."

"Someone on the computer said these things only attack humans, so they'll be okay."

"Dad, you can't just trust people on the internet."

"I know, it's not like he was offering me millions to help him out."

"Okay, Dad."

"There was video of them walking past some

Shetland ponies."

    "Okay, Dad."

    "Well, go get the loader then."

    "Okay, Dad."

    "And stop saying that."

    "Okay, Dad." Josh said with a smile.

    "Annoying little prick."

Nine

The village was acting like nothing was happening, although Sonny suspected the pensioners who were standing outside the village hall were having a good old gossip about it. They glanced his way as he drove past in Josh's orange Ford Ranger. People really didn't like Josh, and Sonny was sure they didn't like him either. Some had even crossed the street when they'd seen him. Despite that he wanted to tell them to get into their homes and not come out until it was safe, but they wouldn't listen to him. Even if he told them about the zombies they'd already encountered they wouldn't believe him, thinking he was smoking that 'wacky-baccy'. Even if he'd had pictures to show them he was sure they'd just say it was something from one of those 'horrible movies'. On a positive note, he wasn't going to have to fight off any zombies by the looks of things.

He pulled into his driveway, before he'd come to a stop she was at the front door.

"Are we seriously doing this?"

"Yeah, Tiffany we are. We've had three on the farm this morning, those folks from the pub last night."

"Okay, we're doing this." Tiffany grabbed a bag from just inside the front door.

They grabbed the other dozen bags that she had packed, dropping them into the back of the Ranger. This was Josh's baby and cleaned much more often than the farm's Defender. It had a load bay liner and a windowed hardtop, and was clean. Tiffany wouldn't have put her stuff in there if it was as dirty as the Land Rover or his Jimny was.

"Is that the Playstation?" Sonny asked.

"What? We could be there a while and Josh has an Xbox. Just be grateful I haven't included my books and movies."

It only took a few minutes for them to load their stuff up and they were on their way back to the farm. As they got out of the main village a police officer on a motorcycle stopped them.

"Where are you all going? There's a curfew in place."

"We know officer, we're just collecting family and going to Holloway farm. It's more secure there," Sonny said.

"Maybe you could tell the idiots in the village that there's a curfew, some of the old biddies are sitting at the bus stop waiting for the bus into town," Tiffany called across from the passenger seat.

"Where's Holloway Farm?"

"It's just off this road a few miles up the road, you would have passed the track that led up to it," Sonny said.

"Okay, go there and do not leave until we have the all clear. This is no laughing matter."

"I know, we've already had zombies up there."

"What? How many?"

"Three, they were staying in the pub and they stumbled into the farm this morning."

"What did you do?"

"We got them penned in a cattle yard, but when the news said how to kill them we did so. Not worth the risk of them getting out."

The officer shook his head. "Go there, stay inside. I'll try and swing back to get more information."

He then sped off towards the town.

"You think the old dears will listen to him?"

"I don't know, but I'd wish I could watch as he

tries,"

Ten

As they ate they watched the panic that was spreading from the Czech Republic. Alec had been sent to eat in the dining room with his grandmother, so had Carrie but she'd argued that she was fifteen and could handle it. She had thrown in if they'd wanted her to 'act her age 'then they should trust her to know what she can take and what she can't.

The German army had deployed along their border with the Czech Republic. Austria, Poland and Slovakia had followed suit quickly which had raised tensions in the region. Australia had stopped all travel into the country except their own citizens, but they would have to enter a quarantine period. Other countries were following their example. The Prime Minister announced at 1pm that all travel to the UK would cease at midnight and flights for British citizens would be provided and get all those holidaying home. The Prime Minister had also said the army was being deployed throughout the country to tackle the growing threat.

All of the major cities and towns in the UK were affected, with London being the worst, but Manchester wasn't far behind. People were fleeing these places at an unmanageable rate but the military were already beginning to block the major roads and forcing cars to turn around. Chaos wasn't a strong enough word to describe what they were seeing from the reporter's cameras.

"That's why it's best to stay put," Frank said.

"Amen to that," Josh said.

"My parents are holding out at my brothers. They had the police banging on doors on their street to check on them," Tiffany said.

"Where are they?" Frank asked.

"Paignton."

"I'd say come here but that's too much of a journey," Josh said.

"Yeah, my brother's house has a six foot fence around most of it, so they think they'll be okay."

"The girls said they're okay?" Frank asked of his two daughters.

"Yeah, their house has that hedge around it. They said if it got worse they'll sneak back but I think they're okay," Madeline said.

"Sitting here getting depressed isn't going to help anyone," Madeline said. "Let's get people into rooms. It'll be tight but we'll all fit in. Sonny, Tiffany, are you okay in the loft?

"I think we'll manage." Tiffany said. The loft had a small living room and bedroom, with its own en-suite.

"Frank, you and Monique can have our room and we'll have the sofa bed in the study."

"No, we'll have the sofa bed. We won't turf you out of your bed, will we Frank?" Monique said from the living room.

Frank started to say something, clearly thought better of it and agreed.

Eleven

After an hour of cursing and long deep breaths from Josh, they got the harvester running and Josh manoeuvred it into the entrance way, then had to back up so Sonny could lock the gate, which they'd forgotten to do. Once it was in though there was barely an inch either side of the header. Normally they'd take the header off the combine to get it in and out because it was so tight. It made a great barrier though.

The rest of the afternoon was spent making sure there weren't any gaps for something to get through. Josh did have a moment where he sighed as they pushed over one of the bulk load trailers. It had been new for this year's harvest and they'd managed to go the whole summer without a dent or a scratch. He turned away as Sonny tipped the trailer on its side, and winced as it clanged against the concrete surface of the yard.

That was the last gap though and the farmyard was secure. He decided he'd check it frequently, thinking better safe than sorry was the best course of action. In the morning they'd move the chickens from where they currently were in his back garden into the small cattle yard. It was on his to-do list anyway, and would give more space in the garden for them if this was to be a long term situation. He had already cleared out any of the blood from the three zombies they had already had to deal with.

Now all they had to do was wait and see how it all played out.

Twelve

Pete and Sonny had volunteered to do overnight watches, with Pete doing the midnight till 6am stint. The house was waking up at that time but it was Frank who took over the watch from Pete, which was basically sitting in the kitchen looking out the window at the farmyard.

Frank had the kettle on and was doing a fry up as Josh and Alec came down. Nothing had happened overnight on the farm, but London had fallen into chaos. The news showed what was happening in the worst hit places. It came with a warning and Alec was sent into the living room before the cameras showed hundreds of zombies dragging people out of cars and begin to pull them apart and start eating them.

The screen cut back to the anchor who looked pale.

"I saw some fucked up shit in the Falklands, but this is beyond anything I've ever seen before," Frank said.

"Anything from Westminster?" Sonny asked.

"Just the same - stay home and wait for further information. The Territorial Army have been fully activated and all emergency services have been called in."

"They waited long enough to do that," Josh said.

"Daddy, what's happening?" Alec asked from the edge of the kitchen.

"Some people are getting very ill, a disease is taking over their bodies and making them hurt other people."

"Are they zombies, Dad??"

"Yeah, I think so."

"So, like The Walking Dead."

"Kind of, have you watched that?"

Alec nodded.

"Carrie lets you watch it doesn't she?"

"No."

"Never play poker, kiddo." Frank said and gave his grandson a hug.

"Are they going to get us?"

"I hope not, we've done a lot to make sure they can't get to us. If they get too close we'll go out and stop them," Frank said.

"They are a long way away from us," Josh said.

"What about the three that were banging on the door?"

The three adults looked at each other for a moment.

"Those people were just a little bit of bad luck. There's been no others near here and we're looking out for others," Frank said as Madeline and Carrie came into the kitchen.

"We're going to have a conversation about letting your seven year old brother watch horror films later that you are not going to enjoy."

Carrie shot her little brother a dirty look.

"He didn't rat you out, but he doesn't have much of a poker face," Frank said.

"Well, we know who's cleaning the bathrooms for the next week," Madeline said.

"This sucks. Dad, you watched RoboCop when you were Alec's age."

"I did, but your grandparents made that decision, not one of your aunts."

"Ah, but you then let Izzy watch it without us knowing." Frank said.

"Ha!" Carrie proclaimed.

"Cheers Dad, appreciate that."

Thirteen

There was a police car at the end of the track. He'd been there for a few minutes before he'd been noticed and was just about to leave when Josh and Frank had driven out of the farmyard and down the track.

"How many of you are up there?"

"Er, nine," Josh said, "What's going on out there?"

"Have you seen any infected?"

"We had three yesterday morning. We got them into a cattle pen and after seeing the news we gave each one a whack on the head."

"Okay, what did you do with the bodies?"

"We burnt them. I didn't want animals eating them."

"Okay, any others around?"

"No, we are keeping a watch."

"How long do you think this is going to last?" Frank asked.

"I can't say. Keep an eye on the news. The armed forces are protecting key infrastructure and have begun to enforce quarantines on the major cities but until things settle down we can't say. How are you for food?"

"We'll be okay for a few days. We've got a few dozen chickens if we get very low."

"If you get a lot of infected then dial 999, but not for anything else. If you get low on food then there's a line being set up for that. I think they're going to do something for going shopping. Keep an eye on the news."

"You be safe," Josh said.

"You too."

Fourteen

Josh shut the gate to the orchard and got back on his quad that was parked next to the one that Sonny was on.

"Hey Josh, check this out." Sonny passed him his phone. Josh hit the play icon on a blank screen. The video played showing a group of the infected somewhere that looked like it might be a Russian city.

People were shooting at the infected but not hitting many, then a snowplow crashed through the twenty or so strong group of dead. The audio filled with cheers as the snowplow turned around and steamed through them again.

"Might be an idea to hook the plow up to one of the tractors?" Sonny said.

"Let's hold fire on that."

"Just use the harvester. Let's see the fuckers get up after that goes over them," Frank said.

Josh and Sonny looked at each other, and smiled.

"I kinda hope we get a horde here now," Sonny said. The orchard had been there for as long as Josh could remember. He remembered stories told to him by his granddad about playing there when he'd been a kid. His family had owned this farm and most of the land for over two hundred years. His sister Beth had done a family tree at school and had got back to 1798 and they'd been on this land then. His children played in this orchard and he hoped his grandchildren would one day as well. Alec had no real interest in the farm, but Carrie did and he thought she'd be the one to take it over when he was ready to hang up his boots. She enjoyed working with the animals but she was starting to show more interest in the machinery and the crops and how the farm was run.

His dad went back to the farm as Josh and Sonny carried on checking the orchard.

Josh and Sonny were on two of the farms quads, or boy's toys, as Frank called them. So far they'd not found anything except the sheep that glared at them for disturbing their peaceful afternoon. But as they came to what had been a gap in the hedgerow they saw the zombie. Years ago this had been a gate out onto a field on the far side but they'd stopped using it as a cut through a few years ago and the hedge wasn't as mature here as it was around the rest of the orchard. It was blocked off with a wooden fence that was this side of the hedge so that any livestock, normally sheep, couldn't get out but because they were smarter than you realise they'd found ways to, so the electric fence had been added, which a zombie was tangled in.

"Do you recognise her?" Josh asked Sonny.

"No, but to be fair, boss, it's kind hard to tell seeing as she's lost her nose and an eye hanging out."

"I reckon you could still tell if you'd known her. You gonna whack it, or shall I?" Josh said.

"I'll let you have this one, and we ain't talking Clark Kent here."

Josh took a deep breath and hit the zombie on the head with the axe handle. They had half a dozen or so axes in the yard so had taken the metal heads off two of them. They were easier to swing without them. The zombie slumped where it was and hung like a marionette doll with slack strings, twitching randomly.

"We should really start keeping count," Sonny said.

"Etch little Z's on our the axe handles, maybe?"

"That's a good idea."

The two men shook hands.

Fifteen

The rest of the orchard was clear and they raced each other back to the farmyard. When they got back the news was reporting that the situation should be under control in the next few days and it wasn't as bad as it looked. People were not to approach the infected unless they had no other choice. After a while of the

Prime Minister calling them 'infected 'a journalist lost his rag and pointed out they were zombies and to stop dressing the matter up. The man was dragged out, questioning the parentage of the two men who were doing the dragging. According to Tiffany this wasn't the first reporter to have been dragged out for this reason.

In the grand scale of things very little was happening. Which Sonny pointed out.

"That's what they said about the First World War. The Phoney War they called it, and we all know how brutal that turned out," Frank said.

"It wouldn't be like that," Sonny said.

"What would it be like?" Madeline said, "Day Of The Dead?"

"The thing about all those films is they're fiction. In real life things are different," Josh said. "For one I can't see zombies taking out tanks in the real world. The army's going to come in heavy and hard and just plough through in their armour and not even get out if there's a horde. I think the Air Force will be ready to bomb them as well."

"But people are still as stupid in real life though. There will be idiots out there that will be going out and counting how many 'kills 'they've made."

Josh and Sonny couldn't help but smile a little as Madeline said those last few words.

"But we're not that stupid, and the government for all their bullshit seem to be on top of this," Frank said. Him and Pete had been out digging more of the moat.

"We're taking precautions though, I mean unless one of us makes a mistake I can't see them getting in," Tiffany said.

"Exactly, sit tight, wait for it to all blow over," Josh said with a wink, a smile and a deep mouthful of tea.

Sixteen

News came through that the zombies were only targeting humans, and the virus hadn't shown any signs of jumping species. Even in cases of scavengers that had been found eating the infected they hadn't shown any signs of turning into zombies. There weren't any cases of the zombies attacking animals but that didn't mean they wouldn't in the future.

After Alec had been sent to bed, and once 9pm had come Sky News started showing footage of the army in action on the streets of London. Josh was impressed with the precision they moved with, and with how much they were wearing. Some of them looked like they were in bomb disposal gear. The first line was armour, mainly smaller tanks and the bigger ones were behind those, and there were armoured cars and Land Rovers in the mix as well. There was infantry but they were keeping back and seemed to be clearing up any stragglers. Even though the street lights were on each of the vehicles had powerful lights mounted on them. They weren't going to get caught unexpectedly.

"Why do you think they started this now? Why not wait till morning?" Madeline said.

"I'd imagine it was because they had the forces in place and didn't want to wait. London's pretty well lit up at night as it is, with those lights it's like daytime," Frank said.

"Time must be a thing as well, right, Dad? I mean the sooner they start getting a handle on it the sooner they'll be able to get it under control," Josh said.

Frank nodded. "That's right, the sooner they start the sooner they get it done."

"Those morons in Parliament don't know what they're doing. They've not exactly got a good track record on being straight with the people," Tiffany said, "Just look at Covid,"

"Oh, they ain't telling us everything. That would be too easy wouldn't it?" Frank said.

"I don't think it's as bad as it looks," Carrie said, "They're not afraid to update us, they said there'd be an update each hour, and there has been."

"Some of which has been pretty trivial though," Sonny said.

"But they have stuck to the hourly update. We've also not lost power, the water is still flowing. Okay we can't go anywhere and the whole country is locked down, but it's not like we're seen hordes of zombies roaming around yet,"

"I think Carrie's right," Josh said, "We always expect the worse but so far not a lot has really happened, well here anyway."

"I think the next twenty-four hours will be important. I do worry that even if it is under control and the military are clearing the major cities then it could be weeks before they get out to smaller communities like ours," Madeline said.

"You're a cheerful sod," Frank said.

"She's got a point," Monique said. "Even when the major cities are getting clearer we'll still be here waiting for them to get around to us."

"Yeah, look how long it's taken to get super-duper broadband out here," Carrie said.

"And we got it sooner than the village because we're closer to the bypass," Madeline said.

Seventeen

Two tedious days passed on the farm. They saw a few zombies mooching about on the main road and in the fields on the other side but none of them moved any closer. Josh quickly realised that as soon as a zombie come up against something it couldn't get past it went a different way.

The news was showing footage of the British Armed Forces working their way through the cities, and keeping martial law with the police. It was also showing hordes of zombies amassing in the smaller cities and towns. These hordes were getting the shit bombed out of them when they were massing if they were away from populations, but they were tearing communities apart in some places. One small town was totally devastated in the space of four hours.

Around the world the zombie outbreak was growing. A few governments were slow in shutting travel down, putting curfews and martial law in place. Others had been much quicker and weren't suffering as much. The Czech Republic was said to be lost. There was no real government control now, the Czech Government had jumped ship and were said to be held up in their embassy in Switzerland. Mainland Europe was devastated. The dead didn't care about borders. They went where they wanted. What was saving the UK from this onslaught was that it was an island. The Channel Islands, for example, were zombie free. As was Australia and much of the Americas. Africa seemed to be fairing well. There were few cases of outbreaks in the Middle East and Far East, but most of the countries outside of Europe quickly shut down travel. Covid had been a hard lesson for some countries and many weren't going to repeat those mistakes. As the days had progressed it was becoming clear that the problem was a European one.

Now Europe was self-imploding there were calls to blow the Channel Tunnel. There were numerous objections to this, mainly from the EU itself. France had even stationed an infantry and an armoured company at the entrance on their side, but this was a source of discontent from some elements in France. The argument being those troops would be of better use in other areas of the country, protecting the French people and not the British. One French politician was even recorded on film condemning the British and saying they'd made their bed when they triggered Brexit.

The tedium was broken a little by Frank and Pete digging the moat around the farm. From what had originally been a moat around the whole farm had turned to just the field on the north side of the farm. On the south side was the orchard and its hedge. The north side of the farm had a four foot stone wall. Behind the farm was another stone wall but that had a pretty dense hedgerow that ran along it..

They were still keeping a watch, even though it was beginning to seem redundant. Izzy had been the first to object to taking a turn but she'd been told if she didn't she'd have to sleep with the chickens.

The next day it all changed. Five zombies chased a man and a child as they ran along the road. The man was in his early thirties, the child couldn't have been more than six years old and he was struggling to carry her and run at the same time.

"I'm going to help," Josh said.

"Me too," Frank said.

"Let's go," Sonny said.

"Don't do anything stupid," Madeline said as the three of them left.

Josh and Sonny had their axe handles, while Frank carried his double-barrelled shotgun.

"Go, I'll catch up," Frank said to the younger men.

Josh and Sonny ran at full pelt along the track that led to the road.

"Over the fence, we've got you." Josh yelled three times until the man heard him. Panic stricken he changed direction, and got to the stone wall and put the little girl over before he climbed over himself, a zombie just missing his hoodie as he did. He grabbed the little girl and started running again. The zombies were trying to get over the fence as Josh and Sonny got to them. The first zombie was almost over the wall before Sonny got to it.

"Head for the farmhouse," Josh shouted as he made his first kill of the day.

They all ducked as a shot rang out. One of the zombie's heads exploded as a second shot rang out. This one knocked the zombie off its feet but was a chest shot. It tried to stand as Frank reloaded the double-barred shotgun.

"Blow their bloody heads off. That'll stop the buggers," Frank said and shot another of the dead.

All of the remaining zombies were the other side of the four foot high stone wall and were out of reach of the axe handles so Frank finished them off before they got any closer, leaving the one he shot in the chest till last. It hadn't been able to get back up but had begun to crawl towards them. Frank blew its brains across the road.

"Thank you, I wasn't going to be able to keep going for much longer," the man said.

"We weren't going to leave you out there, mate," Josh said.

"Not being rude, but you haven't been bitten or anything have you?" Sonny asked.

"No, neither of us have. We had a really decent start but they closed us down. They ain't fast but they never seem to tire." He took a deep breath and then looked around. "We can't stay here. There's thousands coming along that road."

"What do you mean, thousands?"

"Thousands. We've come from town and its overrun. They're following the road, and us. There were a dozen of us when we fled town. I thought we'd lost them, obviously not."

"And now they're coming this way?" Frank said.

"Let's get you two back to the house and then go and check it out," Josh said.

"No, it's not safe here, we need to keep moving," the man said. The little girl with him looked exhausted and scared.

"We're pretty secure here," Josh said.

"No, you're not. They'll get over that wall."

"Not if they don't know we're here," Sonny said.

"They'll smell you, they're like bloodhounds."

"Take a deep breath lad, they won't smell us around all the cow shit," Frank said.

"I'm sorry, but it's not safe. My uncle lives in the village, he's got a motorhome that we're going to get going in and get into the middle of the New Forest."

"Okay, that's up to you. How far are those thousands of zombies?"

"Maybe a couple of miles back."

"Okay, let's give you a lift to the village though. Sonny, you and Tiffany do that and I'll go have a look to see just what's coming."

Peter Germany

Eighteen

With Sonny and Tiffany taking the man and the little girl to the village, Josh headed the other way with Frank in the Defender.

They both had an axe handle and Frank had his shotgun. Josh hadn't got his out of the gun cabinet yet.

"Do you think he was telling the truth?" Frank said.

"We'll know in a minute,"

They turned a corner in the winding country lane and both their mouths dropped. There were easily a thousand zombies walking their way.

"If they walk straight past us, we'll be very lucky. The village doesn't stand a chance though." Frank said.

"We call it in, but we can't just let them come through. We've got to stop them somehow,"

"How do we do that? There's too many to take on just us, we can't barricade the road. The fuckers'll just push their way through the hedges."

Josh looked at the sides of the road which had high hedges either side of them, if something wanted to get through those they could. It would be easy to block the road, they just had to park the harvester on the road, that'll block it off. But they'd just go round it, unless…

Nineteen

"Are you fucking crazy?"

"Mummy said a naughty word," Alec said.

"Yeah Mum, great example you're setting there." Carrie said.

"Don't start," Madeline said, giving them her best mum glare.

"Do you have any better ideas?" Josh said.

"I think it's bloody brilliant," Frank said.

"You are not going to use the harvester to mow them down," Madeline said.

"You heard the operator on the phone. She said to tell people to be quiet and help will be here as soon as they can get it here but they can't give us an estimate," Josh said.

"And that harvester's had it, it was just gonna get scrapped anyway," Sonny said with a smile.

"The more time we argue the less time we have to save the people in the village, they might even keep going up into Meopham,"

"I think you should do it," Monique said. "I've got this horrible feeling that they're going to get us if we don't do something."

"Now I know the world's gone crazy." Madeline shut her eyes for a moment. "What did you have in mind?"

Twenty

"Right, Okay. I get it, but there's not enough of us to do it safely. We need more people." Madeline said. "What if they go through the hedges on the sides of the road? Some will get behind the harvester. You'll need someone there as well. There's only five of you that can go and do something about it. That's not enough."

"I can go, mum." Carrie said.

Josh felt the look that Madeline gave their daughter at her suggestion. Nothing more needed to be said and

Carrie seemed to shrink in on herself a little before looking to her dad to overrule her mother.

"You are not going out there. No chance. You stay here with your mum, brother and Nan. No arguments." Josh tried to give his best 'don't argue on this face 'but he knew it was Madeline's expression that had put to rest Carrie's daft idea.

Sonny clicked his fingers, "The neighbours. PJ and his mate Stefan have been going out and knocking a few heads."

"Bobby and Claire as well." Frank said. "They'll be able to handle this,"

"None of the other landowners will." Pete said. "Most of the villagers are old farts like me or city folk, soft as shite."

"You said that about me when I started," Sonny smiled.

"Aye, you still are. But not as soft as you were,"

"Why Bobby and Claire?" Tiffany said.

"They've already got stuck in, they were in Birmingham with a friend when this all kicked off." Frank said. "They had to fight their way back. Have a look at their car when you can, it's battered to shit."

"There's something about them as well, I wouldn't wanna piss them off," Josh said.

"Even if they agree, that's still not a lot of people."

Josh gave Madeline a hug, "Don't worry, we'll make sure we have vehicles and we all have shotguns. We can handle this,"

Twenty-One

The horde was nearing the farm's entrance as Josh pulled the harvester out onto the road. He started the header spinning.

The old girl had started straight away and hadn't stuttered once.

"You ready, dad?"

"Let's go," Frank was standing on the side of the cab with his shotgun in heavy overalls, goggles, a mask covering his mouth and a hoodie. Everyone was covered from head to toe in something that would be hard to bite through and something to limit the risk of swallowing any blood splatter.

Behind the harvester was Bobby, Claire, and Pete. Bobby and Claire had volunteered to hold that line and Pete had said he'd sit behind them in the Matbro incase they got overrun. He was also keeping an eye on PJ and Stefan incase they needed picking up.

PJ and Stefan were in the field to their left. This one had a more solid hedgerow, which had an old fence running through it from years ago when they had sheep in that field.

That left Sonny and Tiffany in the field to the right of the road. The hedgerow on this side wasn't as mature as the other side and Sonny had one of the tractors with a snow plough attached to the front there incase they got overrun.

Josh lowered the header to ground level and let the header itself spin slowly. He didn't want to dive in too heavy to begin with. Slow and steady would win the race.

The first of the dead walked straight into the turning

blades and were easily pulled under the hauler where the crops themselves would normally be sorted into. He had the header and the hauler spaced as far apart as he could. He knew the header would get clogged up, but he was hoping it would get through the worst of the horde before that. And when that did happen he was planning to just keep going.

The header covered most of the road but there was enough space either side it for something to get through, just. Frank fired a shot.

Bobby and Claire were covering the whole of the space behind them but knew to focus on the right hand side a little more.

"There's more of them than it looked,"

"They might just be more condensed because of the road," Josh said as the harvester began to get into the bulk of the zombies. Josh eased off the accelerator a little as the rota chewed at the wall of dead. It began to tear apart the zombies and body parts began to be tossed around. A hand hit the combines screen right in front of him, and then the blood began to fly.

Twenty-Two

"Stop smilling," Claire said.

"I will if you do," Bobby slapped her on the arse as she poked her tongue out at him.

They had both jumped at the chance of getting stuck in again. They had been going out and killing a few of the dead since they'd got home, and both had loved the idea of seeing a combine getting stuck into the zombies.

"See, this is what those a-holes in Westminster should have done in the first place, but no. They sat around jerking each other off."

"They could have done both, to be fair,"

The first zombie came around the right hand side of the combine. Claire took aim with her shotgun and decapitated it. They both had double barrelled shotguns, but they also had pistols as well. Although those were illegal and hidden, only to be used if they needed to.

The first zombie was followed by two more. Claire shot another one, this time in the chest and reloaded as Bobby shot the third.

"This is going to get very messy." Bobby said.

"Just remember what Josh said, stay away from the chute." Nothing was being spat out the back, yet. And Josh and Frank weren't sure if anything would, but they had warned Bobby and Claire just in case.

Claire adjusted the shortsword on her hip and fired again. She had a collection of swords and thought this would be good if it got hand to hand. Bobby had his grandad's old police trunction that had been used to beat his dad when he'd been a boy, and Bobby's police officer dad had beaten the crap out of him with it as well. Bobby kept it as a reminder of what both men were like, and what he didn't want to become.

Twenty-Three

Zombies came through the hedge as PJ and Stefan knocked their weapons together and jogged towards the three that were heading their way. PJ still carried the hockey stick, while Stefan had abandoned the wheel brace and was wielding a baseball bat he'd found in PJ's garage.

"Dibs on the hipster," PJ shouted and then hit a zombie with a trendy beard, tight shorts and a shirt that was likely bought from some hip shop in Bluewater. "Yeah, boi! Have that!"

"You know this is our apocalypse? We're the two normal, everyday people who become legends after there's an extinction level event. We're going to become zombie hunting legends!"

"What do you mean? Become? We already are!" PJ said as he lined up another zombie, "Hasta la vista, zombie,"

"Noice, delivered perfectly, mate,"

Twenty-Four

Josh had to slow the header down as the combine rolled its way into the condensed horde. They zombies were packed in tight and seemed to be congregating towards the harvester.

The cab was smothered in blood and Christ knows what else, Josh was glad he had the foresight to fill the washer jets up before they'd started.

The header was already bent, twisted, and broken in numerous places but was still turning. The hauler was as well, but Josh knew it'll get clogged soon. It was made to be pulling in grain and rapeseed, not bone, blood and guts.

"God that stinks," Josh said and adjusted his mask.

"I've smelt worse, remember when that cesspit backed up?"

"I do now,"

Franked laughed. He'd had to retreat into the cab to get more ammo. He was also shielding from the blood splatter, but it was easing as Josh had slowed the header down.

"There's more slipping by than I'd like," Josh said.

"They'll be handled, a few the others can deal with, a horde they can't. Keep your eyes on what's ahead of you and we'll see to the rest,"

Twenty-Five

Sonny let the zombie get closer before firing. He wasn't confident with any type of gun, and had only fired one a few times. Josh and Frank had taken him clay pigeon shooting a few weeks ago, and that was the only time he'd handled real gun. Josh and Frank had given him a reminder but he was still a little nervous of the weapon.

He pulled the trigger and clipped the side of the zombie. He fired a second time and this time caught the top of its head, which was enough to stop it moving.

He and Tiffany were doing okay on their side, but more were filtering through a gap in the hedge they'd made and he felt he needed to start shooting to stem the flow so they didn't get overrun.

When they had been in Josh's kitchen planning this out, they had all been surprised when Bobby and Claire had volunteered to cover the rear of the combine. They were expecting this to be where most of the dead that the combine missed would go. Bobby and Claire had also been very adamant that they could handle anything that came their way. There was something about them that made it hard to argue against. On the odd moment Sonny had chanced a glance towards the rear of the harvester he saw they were managing the dead almost too well.

Sonny rested the shotgun on the tractor and weighed in with the axe handle again. Tiffany was swinging hard as well. It was making him proud. She'd thrown herself in with little hesitation, and after she'd killed the first zombie she'd been fine. He was trying to keep an eye on her though, as she wasn't being as aware of her surroundings as he thought she should have been. He realised his mistake at doing this when a zombie grabbed him from behind. He'd been looking towards Tiffany and had lost his own bearings.

He fell backwards and had to scramble to get back to his feet and then push the zombie away as he searched for his dropped axe handle. He grabbed it and wildly and and struck the zombies outstretched arm before Tiffany cracked it over the head.

"Careful, babe,"

"I'm good,"

She gave him a wink and went back to work. She didn't need his help. She had this.

Twenty-Six

"Fuck, bollocks, wanker," Josh spat as the blades finally jammed. The horde was thick here and with the countless dead he had already rundown he was somewhat surprised it had taken this long for the rota to get stuck.

"Dad, get in here for a minute,"

Once Frank was in, Josh put it in reverse and after a moment the blades of the header did start turning back towards the harvester, flicking blood and chunks of zombie towards the cab. They hit the screen and rained down on the top of the harvester. The thudding unnerved Josh, particularly when he took a moment to look at what was hitting the cab. The worse part was the fleshly lump of face with a complete ear that clung to the screen.

The rota wasn't just tossing parts at the harvester, it was flinging them off to the sides as well. Josh had known there would be a clean up needed but the reality of it hadn't hit till now. He didn't like the thought of finding all these body parts that were now tossed willy-nilly around.

"Spin it forward, again. I think it's cleared."

Josh did as his dad suggested and it was. The rota began pulling the dead down towards the hauler again, and now not as much of them was being tossed away from the harvester but downwards.

"I don't think the rota will last much longer, Dad,"

"It's got a bit of life in it yet, when it does give up the ghost just keep going forward."

Frank opened the door and the smell of the dead made Josh gag. Frank just stepped out into it and started shooting again. That man had a cast iron stomach.

The rota clawed its way through the horde that were stumbling forward. Josh kept a better eye on it this time and took a more steady approach as he manoeuvred it around a slight bend in the road.

A thumb bounced off the screen

The harvester started making a pained whine, Josh eased off and focused on the vibrations that were coming through the peddles. She was struggling, the beating heart that was her engine was slowly giving up her last few pulses of life. The horde was beginning to thin though, a few more hundred yards and they'd be through the worst of it. If the rota seized up that was one thing, if the engine gave out now they'd be surrounded by the dead.

"Come on, girl. We've got this," Josh eased off the accelerator and took some pressure off the engine while still keeping the beast moving forward. "Hows the hauler looking, Dad?"

"It's looking alright, most the big bits are getting flung out,"

"Alright, keep an eye on it though,"

Frank looked at Josh, "I'll stick a broom up me arse while I'm at it,"

"Cheers, Dad."

Twenty-Seven

"And he swings, and it's a home run! The Bluejays win the World Series,"

PJ ran around with his arms in the air, clutching the hockey stick he'd used to smash open the head of the zombie that had been in his way.

Stefan was also cracking dead skulls open. They had been going out and knocking the dead over the head since the first morning and had got the hang of getting a head hit in.

"Mate, there's a lot more of them coming,"

PJ looked at the hole in the fence that the zombies had made and were now swarming through. The field was big but suddenly felt very tight as PJ realised there was a dozen of the dead within twenty feet or so of them, which was far too close for them to be able to pick them off easily. The playfulness of the situation bled away and PJ felt his stomach churn and had the sudden urge to pee.

The amount of zombies pushing through the gap in the hedge had widened it and were flowing through, like the Sentinals from The Matrix films. His mortality hit him.

"Fuck it," Stefan said.

PJ looked at the man who had been his friend for as long as he could remember. He saw in his friends eyes what was in PJ's heart, an acceptance that they might not walk away from this.

"For Frodo,"

Stefan smiled, "For Frodo."

The two friends clacked their weapons together and charged towards the growing horde.

Twenty-Eight

Sonny hit the zombie on the head with the butt of the shotgun, then snapped the gun open and pulled the two spent cartages out and slid two more in. He clicked the barrel back into place and fired twice more in quick succession. His nerves dealing with this weapon had gone, the need to be efficient with it forced him to become comfortable using it or they'd die.

Tiffany was still swinging and getting clean hits but they were being pushed back towards where the tractor was.

The dead had realised they were there now and were pressing their way through the gaps in the hedgerow, only a few were getting through but it was a few more than they were able to deal with.

Sonny reloaded the shotgun and fired again. He wasn't getting many headshots but the hits he was getting were enough to knock the dead off their feet and make them less of a threat. Even with this Sonny could see they were on the verge of being overrun. He didn't want to do what they always did in movies and think there was more time than they had.

"Back to the tractor."

Tiffany didn't need telling twice and was off and ten yards ahead of him before he'd had the chance to turn himself.

The zombies had got closer than he'd realised and as he climbed the steps into the tractor one grabbed his leg. It was like a vice and Sonny kicked out as the zombie tried to bite through the two layers of clothing he was wearing, heavy jeans with overalls onto top of them. He was sweating like a pig but the protection was worth the perspiration. But the fear that the zombie would puncture his skin was still there. He kicked harder, more frantically, as Tiffany tried to pull him into the tractor cab. He caught the zombie on the top of the head as it was trying to bite through the fabrics and it jolted the terror. Sonny managed to get his leg free and with Tiffany's help scrambled into the cab and pulled the door shut.

Panic swept across him like a tsunami as he pulled off the overalls and jeans. He didn't think he'd been bitten, but would he feel it? Did the infection take that quickly? Or was his mind shutting off the pain due to the implications of having been bitten? His leg had no marks on it, it was one of the few places on his body he hadn't got fully tatted up yet, and he was grateful for this as his pasty flesh was clear.

"Tell me that's clear?"

"It's clear, babe," Tiffany hugged him and kissed the

top of his head, but had to let go as he climbed to the back window, pushed it open and threw up.

Sonny's body convulsed and didn't stop until he had ran out of anything except bile to purge from himself. He wiped his mouth on his sleeve and pulled the rear window shut. He started taking a few deep breaths, he needed to calm himself down.

Tiffany pulled him into a hug and spoke calming words softly to him as his body dealt with the sudden adrenaline rush.

Outside the dead were climbing over each other to get to the fresh meat they could see but couldn't taste. Sonny watch the dead faces. They weren't even animals. They were more like a fly stuck behind a window, buzzing against glass to get out into the open world again.

Sonny realised he could hear Josh's voice and Tiffany reached up to the radio receiver.

"We're okay, Josh. We're in the tractor. Sonny had a close call but we're both okay. Just a little shaky but we're fine,"

"Alright, drop the plow when you're ready and get stuck in,"

"We will do," Tiffany put the handset back in its cradle. "You okay?"

"Yeah, far too fucking close,"

"I know." She kissed the side of his head.

The clawing of nails on the cab was getting to Sonny.

"Okay, let's get going again,"

He got in the seat and started the John Deere up. He realised his hands were trembling and squeezed them into fists for a moment before lowering the snow plough they had attached to the front of the tractor.

"Hold on,"

The zombies held no resistance to the old tractor's big wheels and once it was rolling anything that had been clambering around it was dragged under. The yellow snow plough was little more than a slightly curved sheet of thick metal that pushed any zombies it hit off to the side.

The fields were dry after a few weeks of no rain and an unusually hot summer, so they wouldn't get bogged down, and the field itself was one that was worked every year so was level. Sonny still took it gently. The fear of toppling it over had set root in his head and he didn't want to risk getting trapped in with it on its side. Somewhere in his head a voice was trying to calm these fears, pointing out the odds of toppling a tractor of this size and weight in a field with little to no obstacles, but that part of his consciousness couldn't shout enough to calm those fears.

The plough itself wasn't going to kill the zombies, unless their heads were hit, but it was doing enough damage to them to mean they weren't able to walk. There were more squeezing their way through the hedgerow now, all in twos and threes from different parts of it. Sonny kept the tractor moving, feeling like he was trying mop up spills from a dam that was slowly beginning to crumble.

Twenty-Nine

"Shit, they're swarming the lads," Frank turned and began firing at the zombies that had flooded into the field where PJ and Stefan were.

Josh felt his heart sinking as he watched the two lads fighting for their lives against more zombies than Josh could easily count. "Eyes forward," he said to himself but put his foot down on the accelerator more. He had to get through this horde quickly so he could turn the harvester into the field, through the hedge, and help the boys.

Thirty

Even with his knee between him and the zombie that had bowled him to the ground, the beast was getting closer to him. PJ had a hand around the monsters neck and the hockey stick between them, and it was still right over his face. Its breath stunk of chicken that had gone off, which was worse than the general rotting meat smell of the zombies themselves. The zombie had a piece of flesh dangling from its braces. He didn't want to know what type of flesh it was, but he knew all the same. He knew fixating on it could lead to his death.

He felt his arm give a little, and he screamed at the zombie out of frustration and fear of death finally snatching him away. But the creature's head flicked to one side and it went limp, then dead weight as it slumped onto him. It wasn't the biggest of bodies but PJ struggled to push the thing off him. He pulled his mask off and vomited. His goggles followed and he had to unzip the overall he had on, and pulled off the straps of the waders. He drew in deep breaths as the world faded in and out for a second. The sound of rapid popping noises brought his head back to the moment.

"Come on, kid," Claire pulled him to his feet and then picked up his hockey stick and gave it to him, "These cunts ain't going to kill themselves." She then gave him a pat on the butt and then began shooting with a pistol. Where'd she get that?

Claire knelt down and continued shooting as PJ got his gear back on and took a deep breath before swinging for the nearest zombie.

Bobby was also shooting with an identical pistol and

that question about who Bobby and Claire Wilson were exactly rang back through his mind.

A yellow farm vehicle steamed through a cluster of zombies, picking them up in the bucket that was mounted at the end of the boom, reversed and then drove forward towards the road and dropped the dozen or so zombies in front of the combine that was still chewing its way through the horde.

"I was born ready, motherfuckers," PJ muttered to himself and began swinging again.

Thirty-One

The combine shuddered, then hesitated for a heartbeat, but then smoothed itself out before Josh had to figure out what the problem was. He was already sweet talking it as he kept it munching its way through the horde. There wasn't far to go, he could see the end of the dead. He wouldn't worry about the stragglers, they could be dealt with by hand, and he thought they had pushed their luck enough with the old girl. He just wanted to park her up and let her rest.

He was ignoring the fields either side of the harvester, especially to his left where the lads were and a large amount of zombies had pushed through. He'd wanted to look when Frank had started cheering, something about Pete in the Matbro, and Bobby and Claire kicking arse.

Josh wanted to look, but he had to kill as many of the dead in the horde still on the road as he could. He was also listening to the harvester. She was talking to him and although she was moving forward well he could hear the engine was slowly giving up. He knew it so well that he picked up anything that wasn't right. He had kept it longer than he normally would have done, because it had never caused him a problem until the end of this last harvest.

"I hear you, girl," he said as he eased back on the accelerator.

The end of the horde was there, barely fifty yards. An abandoned car caused Josh to have to reapply the pressure to the accelerator he'd just taken off. The car was pushed along the road until it got caught on a telegraph pole and a large section of the rear quarter was ripped off and dragged along with the combine as the rest of the car left in the hedge.

The rota finally seized up and then sheered off the rest of the header assembly. Josh cursed as it hung on the hauler but kept going. They were almost there, just keep the old girl moving for a few more seconds.

Then it was done, the horde was gone.

Josh turned the steering gently and the harvester went through the hedge to their left and he got the whole machine into the field and then some before bringing it to a gentle stop.

He grabbed his shotgun and got out. He looked at the battle his family and friends were in before climbing down and joining it himself.

Thirty-Two

PJ smacked the zombie on the back of the head, causing it to fall to the ground and freeing Stefan from its clutches. The blow didn't kill it though, and PJ had to hit it three more times to stop it from trying to get back up.

"Cheers mate, fucker came out of nowhere."

"No worries, dude,"

The two clacked weapons once Stefan picked his up.

PJ noticed there wasn't as many gunshots going off, and looked around. "We've done it. We've stopped them,"

"A bit squeaky bum time there for a moment though wasn't it?"

"I was touching fabric at one point,"

Both laughed and embraced.

Thirty-Three

"I'm glad you'e all okay, I was worried."

"We had it," Bobby said. "We'd appreciate it if word of these stayed between us though." He held his pistol up.

"It's cool, what the man doesn't know won't hurt him," Sonny said.

"The man, really?" Josh said.

"Hey, it fits."

"Does anyone have an idea of how we're going to clear this lot up. Not exactly hygienic is it?"

"The bowsers full, bring it down and wash as much of it away as we can, collect up the bits and put them in the field to be burned."

"The police will be here soon as well, there was a lot of gunfire."

Thirty-Four

When the smell had first hit him, Josh thought he'd never get used to it. As he pulled a leg from the hedge he realised he wasn't bothered by it anymore. Maybe he did inherit his dad's iron gut, or maybe it was the fact he'd pulled more body parts from this hedge than he could count.

They were all still wearing their protective gear, which was making the job harder but they were taking turns in going to the farm for cold drinks.

Bobby and Claire had been the first to mention this and Josh suspected they wanted to go and put their illegal firearms away before the police inevitably showed up.

The next body piece he pulled was an arm, still wearing a Rolex watch that was beyond fucked. It added to the humanity of the situation though, reminding him that these had been people just a day or two ago. The morality of what they had all just done was weighing on him, and he was already feeling the sleepless nights that were coming.

Some of the villagers had come out to watch them clearing up, but it was only a handful and they kept their distance, watching through binoculars for the most part. There were still a few zombies lingering around, mostly trying to crawl after being shredded by the harvester. They were being dealt with as and when they came across them, or if they posed a threat.

They were making good progress with the cleanup and were about a third of the way through when an Army Land Rover drove along the road and parked up near the resting harvester. Half a dozen soldiers jumped out and surveyed the carnage.

Josh, Bobby, Sonny, and Frank walked over to them. Josh saw a sergeant's insignia on one of them. This one took his helmet off, eyed the harvester and then gave them a look that made Josh a little nervous.

"What the fuck is this?"

"Us protecting our families, homes, our livestock, and our community," Frank said. "Major Frank Holloway, Her Majesty's Royal Parachute Regiment, retired."

The sergeant stood a little straighter and his attitude seemed to change. "Were you the ones who called in an approaching horde?"

"Yeah, we were," Josh said.

The sergeant scratched his shaved head. "You had no other choice but to deal with the threat?"

"They would have overrun our homes and the whole village," Frank said.

"Okay, pile up and then burn the bodies and other remains. That as well." He pointed at the harvester. "If you find any forms of ID then store them safely in a sealable container away from anything else. Burn what you're wearing and scrub yourselves until you're red raw. We think the virus can only be transmitted through saliva straight into a wound but we're not a hundred percent on that."

"How long does the infection take to show symptoms?" Bobby asked.

"You'll know about it within three hours. Everyone's different but no one's been observed as taking longer than that."

"And if someone is infected?" Sonny asked.

"Kill them, we don't have a cure. Put them out of their misery before it starts. Off the record, well done. I'll report back that you had no other choice. You're not the first to take things into your own hands." He looked at the harvester, "Well, maybe you're the first to do things this way, but after all is said and done you won't have anything to worry about. The police will be around at some point for details.

The sergeant looked at the mess on the road, "Try and use some form of detergent if you can."

"We've put a load of bleach and shit in the bowser there," Sonny said.

"Good, any other problems, call it in."

One of the soldiers was taking selfies with the combine in the background.

"Will do, Sergeant," Frank said.

The soldiers left and they carried on cleaning up the mess. Josh sent Sonny and Tiffany back to the farm to get some jerry cans that he had full of petrol.

"You know what, boy," Frank said, "Once this is all said and done, I'm gonna have an egg and bacon sarnie,"

They both laughed and carried on cleaning up the mess around them.

I'd like to thank a few people who's support have helped me get to where I am:

Mum, Dad, and my brother. Chrystalyn, Cat, Lynx, Owen, Alice, Louise, Peter, Leanne, Mar, Armand, Chuck, Mary, Stefan, Steph, Jef, Leah, Matty-Bob, Sally, Paul, Jemma, Em, Christopher, Nicola, Adele, and Next Step Nick.

I apologise if I've missed anyone.

Printed in Great Britain
by Amazon